Reference Guide
to Handbooks
and Annuals

(1992 edition)

Reference Guide
to Handbooks
and Annuals

(1992 edition)

**Volumes I-X and
'72-'92 Annuals**

J. William Pfeiffer, Ph.D., J.D.

San Diego • Toronto
Amsterdam • Sydney

PREFACE

The thirty-two books whose contents are classified in this edition of the *Reference Guide* represent nearly 8,000 pages of materials assembled over a period of twenty-three years. These include structured experiences, instruments, lecturettes, theory-and-practice and professional-development papers, annotated bibliographies, and resources. Finding pertinent tools, techniques, and ideas in the *Annuals* and *Handbooks* is made difficult by the serial nature of these publications. Occasionally even the editors of these materials find it frustrating to try to locate a particular structured experience or paper in a hurry. The *Reference Guide* is designed to solve this problem.

Earlier versions of the *Reference Guide* were received so enthusiastically by users of the *Annuals* and *Handbooks* that we at Pfeiffer & Company decided to improve its usefulness and expand its coverage. This edition includes classifications of all the contents of the ten volumes of *A Handbook of Structured Experiences for Human Relations Training* and the twenty-two volumes of the *Annual*. The structured experiences are classified in a way that we think will enhance the user's ability to discriminate among and select from them. There are six major categories and forty-five subcategories. Readers of our older editions will recognize that this classification system, introduced in 1981, is more specific in regard to content and intent.

As in 1990, this edition continues to use the revised classification system for the instrumentation section. This system helps the user find materials more quickly and with more discrimination. The instruments are classified according to what they measure (that is, the focus of the information they provide), *not* according to how they might be used. For example, we would categorize an instrument that deals with individuals' career plans under the general classification of "Personal" and under the subheading of "Life Planning/Career Management"—and not under "Groups/Teams"—even if the instrument would most often be used and discussed in a group setting. The new classification system for the instruments is outlined in the section on instrumentation.

In addition to categorizing contents, we have drawn together much of the material that we have written about the rapidly expanding developments in the human resource field. In the introductions to the sections of the *Annuals* we have treated a number of topics related to the use of structured experiences, instruments, and lecturettes. We have also commented on the shape and progress of theory and research. These useful background materials have been collected and integrated into the *Reference Guide*.

We intend to update this publication periodically to incorporate new material that we have issued. Suggestions for improvement in format and content are welcomed. In this revision of the *Reference Guide* we have again included an article by Brooks E. Smith and John C. Burch on "Decision Effectiveness: A New Way To Introduce the Concept of Commitment into Group Consensus-Seeking Tasks." It follows the "Introduction to Structured Experiences."

We are also interested in continuing to receive manuscripts for possible inclusion in the *Annual*. Users may submit structured experiences, instruments, lecturettes, professional-development papers, and comments on resources available to practicing group facilitators and practitioners of human resource development. We have developed guidelines for contributors that describe how to prepare manuscripts for our review. These guidelines, which were revised in 1992, are included in the 1992 *Annual* and are available on request from our Editorial Department.

The original idea for a reference guide was developed by Rene Robitaille, who was enrolled in the first year of our Laboratory Education Intern Program. I am grateful for his contribution. In addition, I want to acknowledge Steffany N. Parker and other members of the Editorial Department for coordinating this edition.

The *Handbooks* and the *Annuals* now appear in several foreign languages. We are very pleased to be instrumental in making these materials widely available to people who are interested in improving the private and working lives of others. We also are gratified that the number of people who use our materials continues to increase every year. Our publishing aim is to share the useful and valuable information that we collect in the training and development field. It is in this spirit that the *Reference Guide to Handbooks and Annuals* is prepared.

J. William Pfeiffer

San Diego, California

October, 1991

TABLE OF CONTENTS

INTRODUCTION

The *Reference Guide to Handbooks and Annuals* is intended for use by practitioners of human resource development—trainers and group facilitators, organization development consultants, managers, students, and others interested in applied behavioral science. Because the book contains discussions of many facets of adult learning, it can be used as an ancillary text as well as a reference source.

Classifications of each of the types of material included in *A Handbook of Structured Experiences for Human Relations Training, The Annual Handbook for Group Facilitators, The Annual for Facilitators, Trainers, and Consultants,* and *The Annual: Developing Human Resources* are preceded by introductory statements that provide background or related information. These materials have been taken from the introductions to the five sections of the *Annuals.* We have also included in its entirety a paper on design from the 1973 *Annual.*

In each section—structured experiences, instruments, lecturettes, theory-and-practice (now "professional development") papers, and resources—the titles are first organized into appropriate categories according to subject area and then, within each category, listed in order of their publication date. Following these five sections are name and title indices.

This guide can be used in several ways. It can be studied for its information on the technology of human resource development. Trainers and consultants can use it for design ideas for workshops, conferences, meetings, seminars, institutes, and OD or HRD interventions. A particular piece published in one of the *Handbooks* or *Annuals* can be located either by title or by author. Materials related to one another in subject matter, such as structured experiences and instruments in team building, can be cross-referenced.

CLASSIFICATION OF DESIGN COMPONENTS

The chart titled "The Technology of Human Relations Training"[1] illustrates the relationship between learner involvement and the locus of meaning in training. With *experiential* approaches—those that primarily stress active participant involvement versus passive receptivity—the learning is presumably internalized more effectively.

Reading along the bottom of the chart, we see a classification of training design components, ordered according to the extent to which they incorporate learner involvement. The least involving intervention is reading, in which the

---

[1]Based in part on *The Awareness Model: A Rationale of Learning and Its Application to Individual and Organizational Practices* by J. Hall, 1971, Conroe, TX: Teleometrics; and on "How to Choose a Leadership Pattern" by R. Tannenbaum and W.H. Schmidt, May-June 1973, *Harvard Business Review*, pp. 162-164, 166-168.

The Technology of Human Relations Training

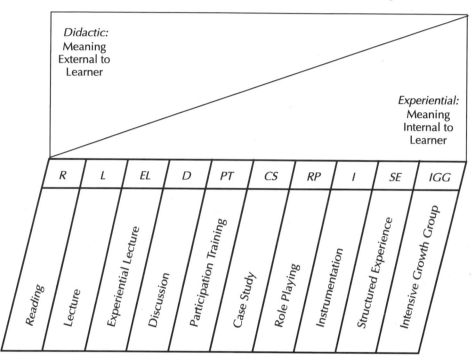

learners are in a *reactive* mode, passively receiving and vicariously experiencing. The most involving intervention is the intensive growth group, in which the learners are encouraged to be *proactive,* to take responsibility for their own learning. In between these two extremes are activities that range from lectures to structured experiences.

The experiential lecture is more involving than the traditional lecture because it incorporates activities on the part of the "audience." Interspersed among the sections of content are brief interactions among participants. These interruptions are designed to personalize the points of the lecture and/or to generate readiness for the next topic.

Discussion is a time-honored teaching intervention that has been extended and refined in participation training. The case-study method, popular in business education, is closely related to role playing, in which a "case" is acted out in a semistructured format.

In instrumentation, which involves learners in self-assessment, the didactic component comes from the theory underlying the items of the scale. Structured experiences stress high participation and "processing" of data generated during interactive activities.

Intensive growth groups are characterized by high learner involvement and interaction. The data for learning come from the life experiences and here-and-now reactions of the group members. Participants are expected to integrate their learning into new self-concepts on their own terms.

The involvement continuum can also be applied to other dimensions, such as risk, self-disclosure, and interaction. Each design component is useful for a different purpose, and there are training situations in which each would be appropriate.

Facilitators are continually faced with the task of planning activities to meet the learning needs of participants. The design problem can be represented graphically as follows:

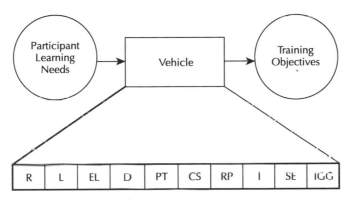

The choice of an effective intervention is made after an assessment of the learning needs of participants and a statement of training objectives. The maturity of the group, the skill and experience of the facilitator, and the environment in which the training takes place determine which approach is used.

AN EXPERIENTIAL MODEL

Experiential learning occurs when a person engages in some activity, looks back at the activity critically, abstracts some useful insight from the analysis, and puts the result to work. Of course, this process is experienced spontaneously in everyone's ordinary living. We call it an *inductive* process: proceeding from observation rather than from a priori "truth" (as in the *deductive* process). Learning can be defined as a relatively stable change in behavior, and that is the usual purpose of training. A *structured* experience provides a framework in which the inductive process can be facilitated. The steps follow those of a theoretical cycle.

The Experiential Learning Cycle

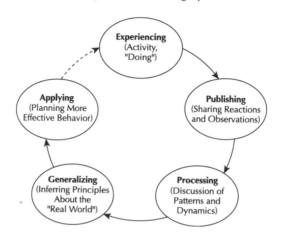

Experiencing

The initial stage is the data-generating part of the structured experience. It is the step that is often associated with "games" or fun. Obviously, if the process stops after this stage, all learning is left to chance, and the facilitator has not completed the task. Almost any activity that involves either self-assessment or interpersonal interaction can be used as the "doing" part of experiential learning. The following are common individual and group activities:

- making products or models
- creating art objects
- writing
- role playing
- transactions
- problem solving or sharing information
- giving and receiving feedback
- self-disclosure

- fantasy
- choosing
- communicating verbally or nonverbally
- analyzing case material
- negotiating or bargaining
- planning
- competing or collaborating
- confronting

These activities can be carried out by individuals, dyads, triads, small groups, group-on-group arrangements,[2] or large groups. Of course, the learning objectives would dictate both the activity and the appropriate groupings.

It is important to note that the objectives of structured experiences are necessarily general and are stated in terms such as "to explore...," "to examine...," "to study...," "to identify...," and so on. Inductive learning means learning through discovery, and the exact things to be learned cannot be specified beforehand. All that is wanted in this stage of the learning cycle is to develop a common data base for the discussion that follows. This means that whatever happens in the activity, whether expected or not, becomes the basis for critical analysis; participants may learn serendipitously.

Sometimes facilitators spend an inordinate amount of energy planning the activity but leave the examination of it unplanned. As a consequence, learning may not be facilitated. It is axiomatic that the next four steps of the experiential learning cycle are even more important than the experiencing phase. Accordingly, the facilitator needs to be careful that the activity does not generate excess data or create an atmosphere that makes discussion of the results difficult. There can be a lot of excitement and "fun" as well as conflict in human interaction, but these are not synonymous with learning; they provide the common references for group inquiry.

Publishing

The second stage of the cycle is roughly analogous to inputting data, in data-processing terms. People have experienced an activity, and now they presumably are ready to share what they saw and/or how they felt during the event. The intent here is to make available to the group the experience of each individual. This step involves finding out what happened within individuals, at both cognitive

---

[2]A group-on-group configuration consists of two groups of participants. One group forms a circle and actively participates in an activity; the other group forms a circle around the first group and observes the first group's activity.

and affective levels, while the activity was progressing. A number of methods help to facilitate the publishing, or declaring, of the reactions and observations of individual participants:

- Recording data during the experiencing stage (putting data "in the can" for later discussion): ratings of such things as productivity, satisfaction, confidence, communication, and so on; adjectives capturing feelings at various points.
- Whips: quick, free-association go-arounds on various topics concerning the activity.
- Subgroup sharing: generating lists such as the double-entry one "What we saw/how we felt."
- Posting/round-robin listing: total-group input recorded on a newsprint flip chart.
- Ratings: developing ratings of relevant dimensions of the activity, tallying and averaging these measures.
- Go-around: systematic "interviewing" of individuals about their experiences during the activity.
- Nominations: variation of the "Guess who?" technique, asking participants to nominate one another for roles they played during the experiencing stage.
- Interviewing pairs: asking one another "what" and "how" questions about the activity.

Publishing can be carried out through free discussion, but this requires that the facilitator be absolutely clear about the differences in the steps of the learning cycle and distinguish sharply among interventions in the discussion. Group members' energy is often focused on staying inside the activity, and they need to be nudged into separating themselves from it in order to learn. (See, for example, the discussion of "de-roling" role players, on page 191 of the 1979 *Annual.*) Structured techniques such as those just listed make the transition from stage one to stage two cleaner and easier. That, after all, is the job of the facilitator—to create clarity with ease.

Processing

This stage can be thought of as the fulcrum, or the pivotal step in experiential learning. It is the systematic examination of commonly shared experience by the people involved. This is the "group-dynamics" phase of the cycle, in which participants essentially reconstruct the patterns and interactions of the activity from the published individual reports. This "talking-through" part of the cycle is critical, and it cannot be either ignored or designed spontaneously if useful learning is to be developed. The facilitator needs to plan carefully how the processing will be carried out and focused toward the next stage, generalizing. Unprocessed data can be experienced as "unfinished business" by participants and can distract them from further learning. Selected techniques that can be used in the processing stage are listed below:

- Process observers: reports, panel discussions (observers are often unduly negative and need training in performing their functions).
- Thematic discussion: looking for recurring topics from the reports of individuals.
- Sentence completion: writing individual responses to such items as "The leadership was...," "Participation in this activity led to...."
- Questionnaires: writing individual responses to items developed for the particular structured experience (for example, see "Motivation Feedback Opinionnaire" in the Structured Experiences section of the 1973 *Annual)*.
- Data analysis: studying trends and correlations in ratings and adjectives elicited during the publishing stage.
- Key terms: posting a list of dimensions to guide the discussion.
- Interpersonal feedback: focusing attention on the effect of the role behaviors of significant members in the activity.

This step should be thoroughly worked through before proceeding to the next. Participants should be led to look at what happened in terms of dynamics but not in terms of "meaning." What occurred was real, of course, but it also was somewhat artificially contrived by the structure of the activity. It is important to keep in mind that a consciousness of the dynamics of the activity is critical for learning about human relations outside the training setting. Participants often anticipate the next step of the learning cycle and make premature generalization statements. The facilitator needs to make certain that the processing has been adequate before moving on.

Generalizing

An inferential leap has to be made at this point in the structured experience, from the reality inside the activity to the reality of everyday life outside the training session. The key question here is "So what?" Participants are led to focus their awareness on situations in their personal or work lives that are similar to those in the activity that they experienced. Their task is to abstract from the processing some principles that could be applied "outside." This step is what makes structured experiences practical, and if it is omitted or glossed over the learning is likely to be superficial. Here are some strategies for developing generalizations from the processing stage:

- Fantasy: guiding participants to imagine realistic situations "back home" and determining what they have learned in the discussion that might be applicable there.
- Truth with a little "t": writing statements from the processing discussion about what is "true" about the "real world."
- Individual analysis: writing "What I learned," "What I'm beginning to learn," "What I relearned."
- Key terms: posting topics such as "leadership," "communication," "feelings," and so on for potential generalizations.
- Sentence completion: writing completions to items such as "The effectiveness of shared leadership depends on...."

It is useful in this stage for the interaction within the group to result in a series of products—generalizations that are presented not only orally but also visually. This strategy helps to facilitate vicarious learning among participants. The facilitator needs to remain nonevaluative about what is learned, drawing out the reactions of others to generalizations that appear incomplete, undivided, or controversial. Participants sometimes anticipate the final stage of the learning cycle also, and they need to be kept on the track of clarifying what was learned before discussing what changes are needed.

In the generalizing stage it is possible for the facilitator to bring in theoretical and research findings to augment the learning. This practice provides a framework for the learning that has been produced inductively and checks the reality orientation of the process. But the practice may encourage dependence on the facilitator as the source of defensible knowledge and may lessen commitment to the final stage of the cycle. The outside information is not "owned" by the participants—a common phenomenon of *deductive* processes.

Applying

The final stage of the experiential learning cycle is the purpose for which the whole structured experience is designed. The central question here is "Now what?" The facilitator helps participants apply generalizations to actual situations in which they are involved. Ignoring such discussion jeopardizes the probability that the learning will be useful. It is critical that attention be given to designing ways for individuals and/or groups to use the learning generated during the structured experience to plan more effective behavior. Several practices can be incorporated into this stage:

- Consulting dyads or triads: taking turns helping one another with back-home problem situations and applying generalizations.
- Goal setting: writing applications according to such goal criteria as specificity, performance, involvement, realism, and observability (see the 1972 *Annual,* pages 133 and 134).
- Contracting: making explicit promises to one another about applications.
- Subgrouping: in interest groups, discussing specific generalizations in terms of what can be done more effectively.
- Practice session: role playing back-home situations to attempt changed behavior.

Individuals are more likely to implement their planned applications if they share them with others. Volunteers can be asked to report what they intend to do with what they have learned, and this can encourage others to experiment with their behavior also.

It is important to note that on the diagram of the experiential learning cycle there is a dashed arrow from "applying" to "experiencing." This is meant to indicate that the actual application of the learning is a new experience for the participant, to be examined inductively also. What structured experiences "teach," then, is a way of using one's everyday experiences as data for learning about human interactions. This is sometimes referred to as "relearning how to learn." Actually, there are other ways to learn. For example, skills are best learned through practice toward an ideal model, knowledge of results, and positive reinforcement. Also, structured experiences do not readily facilitate the development of large-scale perspective; lecture-discussion methods are probably superior for such a purpose. What experiential learning does accomplish, though, is a sense of ownership over what is learned. This is most easily achieved by making certain that each stage of the learning cycle is developed adequately.

REFERENCE

Jones, J.E., & Pfeiffer, J.W. (Eds.). (1973). *The 1973 annual handbook for group facilitators.* San Diego, CA: Pfeiffer & Company.

A GLOSSARY OF TERMS IN EXPERIENTIAL TRAINING

Trainers and group facilitators are notorious for their use of jargon. Those who use an "applied-behavioral-science" approach often use technical terms interchangeably, adding to the confusion of participants. The following listing is intended to help clarify this situation.

Activity	A design for participation to create a common experience to be studied and discussed by participants.
Case Study	Group discussion and problem solving from material about an actual situation.
Critique	Group evaluation of the effective and ineffective aspects of a learning design.
Deductive	A learning method that begins with "truth" and proceeds to its logical conclusions.
Design Task	An assignment to create a plan for learning through interaction.
De-Roling	Helping participants in a role play to extricate themselves from their assigned roles and to resume their normal interactions.
Didactic	Adjective describing a teaching approach in which information is imparted from an expert.
Energizer	Activity designed to develop readiness for participation in learning events; usually involves physical movement and fun.
Exercise	Repetitive activity, usually designed as a part of training to develop skills.
Experience-Based	Synonymous with "Experiential."
Experiencing	Phase I of the "Experiential Learning Cycle"; a learning activity to be discussed by participants afterwards.

Experiential	Adjective describing an approach to learning in which participants in an activity learn through reflection on the activity itself.
Experiential Learning Cycle	A model of an inductive learning process consisting of five phases: Experiencing, Publishing, Processing, Generalizing, and Applying.
Experiment	A (structured) activity with unpredictable outcomes.
Facilitation	Helping participants to learn from an activity; conducting experiential training.
Facilitator	A person who uses experiential methods to promote learning; literally, "one who makes things easy."
Feedback	Information about the effects of one's behavior.
Game	An activity that is engaged in for its own sake; usually connotes fun and competition or chance.
Ice Breaker	An activity to help participants to release anxiety at the beginning of a training event; usually fun, involving becoming acquainted with one another.
Inductive	A learning method that is based on the discovery of "truth" from the examination of experience.
Input	Exposition of information or theory; contribution to a discussion.
Instrument	Paper-and-pencil device used to inventory or rate oneself or a system.
Instrumentation	The use of instruments in training or research.
Intensive Growth Group	Unstructured experience focused on the "here and now"; may be T-group, encounter, therapy, counseling, or marathon.

Item	A component of an instrument.
Likert Scale	Type of attitude-measurement scale developed by Rensis Likert; usually "strongly agree, agree, undecided, disagree, strongly disagree."
Model	(1) Theoretical explanation of a complex set of phenomena; (2) ideal behavior type.
Modeling	(1) Demonstrating effective behavior; (2) developing a theoretical explanation of a process.
Norms	(1) Expected behaviors; (2) statistical summary of responses to an instrument.
Package	A self-contained training design that is completely developed, with little or no flexibility.
Parameter	Characteristic factor, goal, or limitation; what the facilitator has to work with in creating a learning design.
Participation Training	Group discussion that includes learning how to be a more effective group member.
Processing	Group discussion of the results of a learning activity; Phase III of the Experiential Learning Cycle.
Publishing	Sharing reactions and observations; talking about one's experience during a learning activity; Phase II of the Experiential Learning Cycle.
Questionnaire	An instrument that does not have correct answers; used in surveys.
Reinforcement	Anything that raises the probability that a response will be repeated.
Response Format	A scale or method used by participants in reacting to the item of an instrument.

Role Playing	A design for learning in which participants act out a situation through assigned parts that they play spontaneously.
Self-Assessment	Looking inward at oneself, usually through a learning activity.
Self-Disclosure	Communicating about oneself to others; usually connotes letting others know about one's private self.
Set	Psychological condition prior to an activity; attitudinal predisposition; expectations.
Simulation	Interactive learning package designed to re-create or mirror a larger, more complex situation in order to sponsor learning.
Skill Building	Developing effective behavior through practice toward an ideal type, with both knowledge of results (feedback) and reinforcement.
Structured Experience	A design for inductive learning through the implementation of the Experiential Learning Cycle; focuses on particular learning goals.
Test	An instrument with "correct" answers.
Win-Lose	Adjective describing a competitive situation in which there must be a loser in order for there to be a winner.

Although these terms are not technically precise, we have found it useful to insist on making sharp distinctions between them for the sake of clarity and ease of comprehension. Undoubtedly many persons would argue for even more specific and exclusive definitions. We invented the term "structured experience," for example, to emphasize the two aspects of that intervention: the existence of some boundaries and the process of learning through doing.

INTRODUCTION TO STRUCTURED EXPERIENCES

Structured experiences—designed to focus on individual behavior, constructive feedback, processing, and psychological integration—are infinitely varied and variable. They can be adapted easily to the particular needs of the group, the aim of a training design, or the special competencies of the training facilitator. In publishing structured experiences, we assume that facilitators are, by their nature, innovators. As one friend remarked, "I use your materials all the time, but I almost never do things the way you describe them."

We are concerned that all human-interaction training experiences have adequate processing so that the participants are able to integrate their learning without the stress generated by unresolved feelings or a lack of understanding. It is here that the expertise of the facilitator becomes crucial. If the structured experience is to be responsive to the needs of the participants, the facilitator must be able to assist the participants in successfully processing the data that emerge from that experience. Thus, an activity should be selected on the basis of two criteria—the facilitator's competence and the participants' needs.

CONSIDERATIONS IN DEVELOPING A STRUCTURED EXPERIENCE

To further the creation and availability of these valuable materials, we are including some points and questions to be considered when developing a structured experience.

Goals. These should be limited in number and stated in language that participants can understand. A good goal is *specific* in that it states exactly what will occur; it is less specific in terms of the result of that occurrence, in order to permit inductive learning, i.e., learning through discovery. For example, a goal may be "to examine" or "to explore" the effects of collaboration and competition. The activity will involve those two dynamics. What is learned, however, may differ from participant to participant, depending on the participants' backgrounds and their unique experiences during the activity. A goal is *performance oriented,* to guide the person toward what he or she is going to *do;* it *involves* the individual in the goal objective; it is *observable,* so that other people can see the result; and, most important, it is *realistic.* For maximum effectiveness, a goal must be attainable.

Group Size. The minimum and maximum number of participants, the optimum size of the group, and the number and size of subgroups should be noted where relevant. If there are extra participants, how should they be utilized? (They could, for example, be designated as observers or added to subgroups.)

Time Required. This should be a realistic expectation, based on actual trials of the experience. Adequate time must be allowed for sharing and processing the learnings. If the experience requires a long period of time, can it be divided into more than one session?

Materials. The criteria here are easy availability, utility, and uncomplicated preparation. The specific forms, sheets of information, or work sheets needed and the quantities of each should be listed. If appropriate, an observer sheet should be devised for the activity. Audiovisual aids (such as felt-tipped pens, newsprint, sound or film equipment), pencils and paper, and any other special materials should be indicated if applicable.

Physical Setting. What are the participants' needs: Must groups be private, quiet, isolated? Do participants sit around tables or on the floor? Do they need writing surfaces? Can the experience take place outdoors? Do rooms need to be specially designated or arranged for certain groups or subgroups? Easily movable furniture is usually desirable to aid in the flexibility of the group.

Process. This is a step-by-step procedure that should indicate what the facilitator does and says and what the participants do in the appropriate sequence. The beginning and end of each step should be specified. A time estimate may be useful for each step or phase.

Variations. Adaptations may be noted to vary the activity's content, sequence, use of observers, time for each step, materials, size of groups, complexity of process, and use with intact groups.

Credit Line. Ideas and designs of others should be acknowledged; if there is more than one author to be credited, the authors' names should appear in the order of the significance of their contributions, the senior author or contributor listed first.

Work Sheets. These should be designed and written so that they contain sufficient room in which the participants may write, are simple and easy to reproduce, have clear instructions, and are necessary and meaningful to the activity. Whenever possible, each work sheet should be on one page, with type large enough to read easily. It is practical to have the work sheet contain its own instructions. If it does not, it should tell the participant that the facilitator will give oral instructions. Sources for work sheets should be acknowledged.

Handouts. This format is especially useful for a discussion of the theory underlying new behavior suggested by the structured experience. Unless necessary, participants should not be allowed to read handout materials while the process is running. However, if handouts are to be provided, the participants should be told at the beginning of the experience so that they will not prepare to take notes.

CONSIDERATIONS IN USING A STRUCTURED EXPERIENCE

Certain questions need to be asked by the facilitator who is contemplating using a structured experience as an intervention in a training event. This set of considerations constitutes a self-examination that is intended to help the facilitator select and develop designs that are both relevant and effective.

What are the goals of this group and why was it formed? Structured experiences are designed for a variety of purposes, but their most effective use is within programs that are aimed at specific learning goals. The facilitator needs to keep these goals in mind at all times.

At what stage is the group in its development or what stage is it likely to reach? Different issues surface at various stages of group development, and some activities are particularly useful at some points in group life. A feedback design may be inappropriate in the earliest stages but highly beneficial after the group has a brief history.

What is my contract with the group? Some groups expect the facilitator to "run" everything. It is important to minimize the gap in expectations between the facilitator and the participants. Using too many structured experiences may reinforce dependency on the part of the members, and they may turn to the facilitator to introduce an activity rather than confronting their own behavior. The facilitator needs to make it clear that each member is responsible for his or her own learning.

Why is it important that I intervene? Because it is possible for facilitators to meet their own needs at the participants' expense, it is important that they assess their own motives for intervening into the interaction among members. Useful distinctions can be made between making things happen, letting things happen, and being a part of what is happening. One useful thought is "When in doubt, wait."

Why does this particular intervention appeal to me? It may be that the structured experience seems appropriate because it would be "fun" to do, but the overriding consideration should be the learning needs of the participants at a particular point in the group's development. One should be careful not to overuse any given activity; this might indicate that the facilitator has "a solution in search of a problem."

How ready are these participants to take risks, to experiment? Some structured experiences, such as guided fantasies and nonverbal activities, are threatening to many participants and may evoke anxiety and defensiveness rather than openness to learning. It is useful, however, to establish an experimentation norm in laboratory education, and participants should be expected to "stretch" somewhat.

What content modifications can I make for an effective, appealing design? Local issues and concerns can be incorporated into structured-experience materials and processes in order to heighten the possibility of the transfer of training. Such advance preparation can have a high payoff in developing work norms and avoiding "game playing." Roles, goals, company policies, issues, cases, etc., can be gathered with the help of participants. The article "Decision Effectiveness: A New Way To Introduce the Concept of Commitment into Group Consensus-Seeking Tasks" by Brooks E. Smith and John C. Burch, which follows this introduction, presents a way of adapting many consensus-seeking tasks so that both accuracy and commitment can be objectively measured.

What advance preparations need to be made? Appropriate rooms, with the right kinds of furniture and equipment, should be scheduled. The staff may need to be prepared. Materials must be duplicated and assembled. Sometimes it is helpful to prearrange the furniture so that participants are seated in preparation for the first phase of the process.

How rigid are the time restraints for the session? It is necessary not to generate more data than can be adequately processed within the session. It is better not to use an activity than to leave too much data "hanging" at the end. One consideration is to anticipate which elements of the design can be speeded up or expanded, if necessary.

How am I going to set up the processing? Since the processing of the data generated by the structured experience is more important than the experience itself, this planning phase should be carefully considered. A number of strategies can be used, such as process observers who have been briefed and who are using comprehensive guides; lecturettes; instrumented processing with brief questionnaires; subgrouping; the empty chair or group-on-group techniques; and interviewing. Some of the data may be saved for use in later training designs.

How am I going to evaluate the effectiveness of the design? Because structured experiences are best employed in an atmosphere directed toward specific goals, some assessment of the extent to which the goals of a given activity were met is necessary. Such a study may be impressionistic and/or "objective," but it needs to be planned beforehand. The facilitator needs to decide the basis for judging whether or not or to what degree the aims of a particular intervention were accomplished.

FAILURE OF STRUCTURED EXPERIENCES

Structured experiences can "fail" That is, they may not produce the predicted results, or they may produce unexpected results.

Usually, such failure occurs when the experiential model is truncated or abbreviated or when it is inadequately implemented. Each step in the model is an essential part of the entire sequence; each needs sufficient attention to effect its full impact. Inadequate processing is the most common cause of the failure of the model.

Unfortunately, failure on the part of any facilitator only increases the chances that other facilitators may encounter difficulty in their attempts to present a structured experience. If participants in a learning activity have previously had ineffective training experiences, it is likely that they will be more resistant to, and less inclined to involve themselves in, future training experiences.

Thus, the question of the "failure" of structured experiences becomes significant. Failure promotes subsequent failure. For this reason, we are stressing here the need for facilitators to confront the demands and requirements of the experiential model so that they—and their colleagues who follow them—may gather the rewards and benefits the model offers.

The implications of the model stress the necessity for adequate planning and sufficient time for each step. An appropriate structure is especially important for processing, generalizing, and applying. When handled with care, concern, and skill, the experiential approach is invaluable for group facilitators in the fields of applied behavioral science and organizational training and development.

NUMBERING OF STRUCTURED EXPERIENCES

The structured experiences are numbered consecutively throughout the series of *Handbooks* and *Annuals*, in order of publication of the volumes. The following list specifies the numbers of the structured experiences to be found in each publication in the Pfeiffer & Company *Handbooks* and *Annuals*.

Structured Experience	Publication
1 through 24	Volume I, *Handbook*
25 through 48	Volume II, *Handbook*
49 through 74	Volume III, *Handbook*
75 through 86	1972 *Annual*
87 through 100	1973 *Annual*
101 through 124	Volume IV, *Handbook*
125 through 136	1974 *Annual*
137 through 148	1975 *Annual*
149 through 172	Volume V, *Handbook*
173 through 184	1976 *Annual*
185 through 196	1977 *Annual*
197 through 220	Volume VI, *Handbook*
221 through 232	1978 *Annual*
233 through 244	1979 *Annual*
245 through 268	Volume VII, *Handbook*
269 through 280	1980 *Annual*
281 through 292	1981 *Annual*
293 through 316	Volume VIII, *Handbook*
317 through 328	1982 *Annual*
329 through 340	1983 *Annual*
341 through 364	Volume IX, *Handbook*
365 through 376	1984 *Annual*
377 through 388	1985 *Annual*
389 through 412	Volume X, *Handbook*
413 through 424	1986 *Annual*
425 through 436	1987 *Annual*
437 through 448	1988 *Annual*
449 through 460	1989 *Annual*
461 through 472	1990 *Annual*
473 through 484	1991 *Annual*
485 through 496	1992 *Annual*

DECISION EFFECTIVENESS: A NEW WAY TO INTRODUCE THE CONCEPT OF COMMITMENT INTO GROUP CONSENSUS-SEEKING TASKS

Brooks E. Smith and John C. Burch

Group decision making or consensus seeking has occupied a prominent place within management literature in recent years. A host of articles and presentations have supported the use of group decision making. Many models—some simple, some complex—have attempted to show how and when to seek consensus. Irrespective of the arguments or the model, commitment and quality of decision emerge as major factors associated with effective consensus seeking. Yet, when one examines the wide array of tasks used to teach consensus seeking, it becomes obvious that the activities and/or experiences are strongly oriented to the quality or accuracy of the decision with little regard to looking at—much less measuring—the degree of commitment within the group.

This article presents a way of adapting many consensus-seeking tasks so that both accuracy and commitment can be objectively measured, and it examines a typical consensus-seeking task.

TYPICAL CONSENSUS-SEEKING TASK

As an example, "Lost at Sea: A Consensus-Seeking Task"[1] will be examined. This structured experience, published by Pfeiffer & Company, is not only representative, but it is widely known and used. Figure 1 presents instructions for completing the task, and Figure 2 provides a work sheet that incorporates the steps that are generally followed.

After the individual and group work has been completed and the correct ranking has been given, participants compute an individual score and a team score, both of which objectively measure the quality or accuracy of the decision—and do it well. However, the purpose of consensus seeking is not just to achieve the best or most accurate answer. What we are really concerned with is whether the decision will work to achieve our goals. To answer this question we must look at the concept of decision effectiveness.

---

[1] *The 1975 Annual Handbook for Group Facilitators* (pp. 28-34). San Diego, CA: Pfeiffer & Company. *Lost at Sea*, a consensus-seeking task based on this structured experience, was also published in 1989 by Pfeiffer & Company as a booklet for individual participants and may be purchased along with a *Leader's Manual.*

DECISION EFFECTIVENESS

Decision effectiveness is the degree to which a given decision, once implemented, achieves the goal or goals. As such, decision effectiveness is a function of the relationship between the quality or accuracy of a decision and the degree of commitment toward that decision. In some situations, the quality or accuracy of the decision may be very important, even critical. Suppose a management team is expanding production and has decided to build a new plant. Many of the decisions in this situation are critical, and the quality of the decisions is vital to the success of the company. On the other hand, suppose the management team has three proposals for new products that are so similar in respect to all the variables being considered that they are basically equal. In this case, the quality of the decision about which of the three is chosen or given priority may not be important to the success of the company.

However, even if the quality of the decision is not important, whether or not the people involved truly accept a given decision and are really committed to implementing it could be critical. For example, if a decision were made to reorganize a portion of the company, acceptance and commitment could play a very important role in the success of the reorganization. On the other hand, if a decision were made to change the company's insurance carrier—while providing the same benefits—commitment and acceptance may have little to do with whether the change is successful.

Instructions: You are adrift on a private yacht in the South Pacific. As a consequence of a fire of unknown origin, much of the yacht and its contents have been destroyed. The yacht is now slowly sinking. Your location is unclear because of the destruction of critical navigational equipment and because you and the crew were distracted trying to bring the fire under control. Your best estimate is that you are approximately one thousand miles south-southwest of the nearest land.

Below is a list of fifteen items that are intact and undamaged after the fire. In addition to these articles, you have a serviceable, rubber life raft with oars large enough to carry yourself, the crew, and all the items listed below. The total contents of all survivors' pockets are a package of cigarettes, several books of matches, and five one-dollar bills.

Your task is to rank the fifteen items below in terms of their importance to your survival. Place the number *1* by the most important item, the number *2* by the second most important, and so on through number *15*, the least important.

[The participant assumes (a) that the number of survivors is the same as the number on his or her team, (b) that the team members are the actual survivors, and (c) that all items are in good condition. Each participant first works individually to rank each item without discussing the situation with the other members of the team. After that task is completed, the team discusses the situation and arrives at a team ranking. Once the team discussion begins, no one is allowed to change his or her individual ranking.]

Figure 1. Instructions for Lost at Sea Activity

ITEMS	STEP 1 Your Ranking	STEP 2 Team Ranking	STEP 3 Correct Ranking	STEP 4 Difference Between Steps 1 & 3	STEP 5 Difference Between Steps 2 & 3
Sextant					
Shaving mirror					
Five-gallon can of water					
Mosquito netting					
One case of U.S. Army C rations					
Maps of the Pacific Ocean					
Seat cushion (flotation device approved by the Coast Guard)					
Two-gallon can of oil-gas mixture					
Small transistor radio					
Shark repellent					
Twenty square feet of opaque plastic					
One quart of 160 proof Puerto Rican rum					
Fifteen feet of nylon rope					
Two boxes of chocolate bars					
Fishing kit					
TOTALS				Your Score	Team Score

Figure 2. Lost at Sea Work Sheet

Thus, as a general working rule, we can say that decision effectiveness is a function of the quality of the decision plus commitment, or:

$$DE = f(Q + C),$$

where DE = Decision effectiveness

Q = Quality or accuracy of decision

C = Commitment or acceptance

Based on this rule, the better the quality or accuracy of the decision and the higher the degree of commitment, the greater the probability that a given decision, once implemented, will attain the goal or goals. Given the above, the next question is "How do we introduce this concept into consensus-seeking tasks?"

HOW TO ADAPT CONSENSUS-SEEKING TASKS

Returning to the "Lost at Sea" example, we begin the adaptation by changing Figure 2 to the modified work sheet in Figure 3.

Figure 3 adds two new columns. The one now labeled "Step 3" is called "Your Second Ranking." After the group has completed the individual work and the team work, but before the correct answer is distributed, the group is given the following instructions:

> You now have a team ranking, but you may or may not be in complete agreement with it. Although you might have received some valuable information in the discussion with your team members, assume that you alone must now rank the fifteen items in terms of their importance to your survival. Place this ranking in the column headed "Your Second Ranking."

The participants then rank the items individually for the second time and enter their answers in column 3. Participants are then asked to derive the absolute difference between the numbers in column 2 ("Team Ranking") and column 3 ("Your Second Ranking") and enter the differences in column 4. The numbers in column 4 are then totaled in the block at the bottom ("Your Acceptance Score"). The acceptance score is an objective measure of each individual's commitment to the decision. The lower the acceptance score, the higher the commitment to the group ranking; the higher the acceptance score, the lower the commitment. The rationale is that if the participant completely accepted the group decision, his or her second ranking would be the same as the team ranking. However, if participants are not completely in agreement with the team, their second rankings should differ from the team ranking. Therefore, the difference between the team score and the second individual ranking is a measure of the individual's acceptance or commitment to the decision.

ITEMS	STEP 1 Your First Ranking	STEP 2 Team Ranking	STEP 3 Your Second Ranking	STEP 4 Difference Between Steps 2 & 3	STEP 5 Correct Ranking	STEP 6 Difference Between Steps 1 & 5	STEP 7 Difference Between Steps 2 & 5
Sextant							
Shaving mirror							
Five-gallon can of water							
Mosquito netting							
One case of U.S. Army C rations							
Maps of the Pacific Ocean							
Seat cushion (flotation device approved by the Coast Guard)							
Two-gallon can of oil-gas mixture							
Small transistor radio							
Shark repellent							
Twenty square feet of opaque plastic							
One quart of 160-proof Puerto Rican rum							
Fifteen feet of nylon rope							
Two boxes of choco-late bars							
Fishing kit							
TOTALS							
				Your Acceptance Score		Your Score	Team Score

Figure 3. Modified Lost at Sea Work Sheet

At this point in the experience, a lecturette on the concept of decision effectiveness is helpful. After the lecturette, the participants are asked to share within their groups their acceptance scores and the reasons for those scores. After the discussions, the correct answers are distributed. Participants then complete steps 5, 6, and 7 and enter the totals for steps 6 and 7 at the bottom of the work sheet. The numbers for "Your Score" and "Team Score" are measures of the quality or accuracy of the decision. The lower these scores, the higher the quality or accuracy of the decisions.

At this point, each team can calculate an average acceptance score by totaling the acceptance scores for all members of the team and dividing by the number of members in the team. The average acceptance score and the team score can then be plugged into the decision-effectiveness formula discussed earlier:

$$DE = f(Q + C)$$

In the "Lost at Sea" example, the most effective team (i.e., the team that has the highest probability of attaining its goal) is the team with the lowest decision-effectiveness score.

CONCLUSION

Most consensus-seeking tasks focus on the quality or accuracy of the decision and ignore the equally important aspect of commitment. By introducing the concept of decision effectiveness and by adding a second individual ranking after the group has reached a team decision, both accuracy and commitment can be objectively measured in many consensus-seeking tasks.

Editor's Note: On pages 120-124 of this *Reference Guide* is a list of the consensus-seeking activities published in the Pfeiffer & Company *Annuals* and *Handbooks*.

Brooks E. Smith, Ph.D., is associate professor of management and coordinator of graduate business studies at the University of Southern Mississippi—Gulf Coast in Long Beach, Mississippi. He is also a management consultant and motivational speaker and has published a number of articles in the area of self-development and organizational behavior.

John C. Burch, Ed.D., is associate professor of management and coordinator of management studies at the University of Southern Mississippi—Gulf Coast in Long Beach, Mississippi. He is also a management consultant and has published in the area of organizational behavior.

CLASSIFICATION OF STRUCTURED EXPERIENCES

THE NEW FORMAT

Professionals who use the structured experiences in the *Handbooks* and *Annuals* have long sought an easy, reliable way to choose appropriate activities for particular training events. To meet this need, we have classified[1] the 496 structured experiences in this *Reference Guide*—all the structured experiences previously published in the ten volumes of the *Handbook* and the twenty-one volumes of the *Annual*—into the following six major categories, based on the *goals* of the experience:

- Personal: activities that focus on the expansion of personal insight, awareness, and development of interpersonal skills.
- Communication: activities that emphasize verbal and nonverbal communication skills, especially in interpersonal and intragroup relationships.
- Group Characteristics: activities that examine how individuals affect group functioning.
- Group Task Behavior: activities that focus on how groups organize and function to accomplish objectives.
- Organizations: activities that help individuals and groups function within an organizational context.
- Facilitating Learning: activities that create a climate of responsiveness and encourage skill development.

Each major category has been divided into subcategories in order to help the trainer to select activities with a high degree of precision. The same subcategories may be included under more than one major category; for example, "values clarification" appears under "Personal" and under "Group Characteristics." Of course, structured experiences may be used for any number of goals other than those indicated, but by using this categorization, the professional trainer will greatly increase the likelihood of finding experiences that have been designed to meet his or her particular goals. It is true that a sophisticated classification system necessarily involves fine distinctions about the placement of a particular activity. The primary intent of this system is to help the user to find materials quickly and with discrimination. We support and encourage facilitators in developing their own cross-referencing systems for the use of activities.

Definitions of the subcategory topics within major categories follow.

---

[1]We would like to acknowledge the contributions of Peter Rutherford to the conception and planning of this category system.

Personal

Self-Disclosure: activities that teach the ability to reveal oneself to others.

Sensory: activities that focus on personal awareness and skills through the exploration of the senses.

Feelings Awareness: experiences that focus on emotional understanding of oneself.

Feedback: activities that promote awareness of others' ability to increase one's understanding of self and that encourage acceptance of the opinions or feelings of others.

Assumptions: activities that help one to see that the assumptions he or she may make about others may significantly influence perceptions.

Values Clarification: activities that clarify the process by which one chooses, prizes, or acts.

Life/Career Planning: activities that allow one to evaluate the present and future of one's career or life.

Communication

Communication Awareness Experiments: activities that illustrate what happens when two people communicate, either verbally or nonverbally.

Developing Interpersonal Trust in Dyads: activities that help two people to develop a personal or work relationship.

Sexual Awareness: experiences that expand awareness of and skill in handling the sexual aspect of relationships.

Listening: skill-building activities that help people to listen actively.

Interviewing: activities to develop skills needed in the two-person interview situation.

Assertion: activities that improve people's ability to affirm their own positions while being sensitive to the needs of others.

Group Characteristics

Process Observation/Awareness: activities that help to develop skills in observing what is taking place in a group.

Leadership-Membership: activities that deal with issues of power, leadership style, motivation, and leaders' and members' interactions with one another.

Communication: activities that offer practice in group communication.

Values Clarification/Stereotyping: activities to illustrate the effects on the group of individuals' personal values and their stereotypes or prejudices.

Group Task Behavior

Problem Solving/Awareness: activities that develop skill in and awareness of problem-solving techniques.

Generating Alternatives: activities to practice an early creative step of the problem-solving process.

Group Feedback: activities that develop awareness of and skills in group feedback.

Competition (Win-Lose): activities that involve competitive behavior by group members and explore its effect on the accomplishment of a task.

Competition and Collaboration (Win-Lose and Win-Win): activities that deal both with the competitive tendencies that emerge within groups and the appropriateness of collaborative behavior.

Collaboration (Win-Win): activities that deal with only the cooperative aspect of group task behavior.

Conflict Resolution/Values Polarization: activities that develop skills to deal with conflicts in the group because of differing values of members.

Consensus/Synergy: activities to develop the group's skills at reaching general agreement and commitment to its decisions and goals.

Organizations

Awareness/Diagnosis: activities that help people to be aware of the forces that affect the functioning of their organizations and to learn to diagnose organizational problems.

Team Building: learning experiences to develop the effectiveness of teams within an organization.

Decision Making/Action Planning: activities that teach these necessary skills within organizations.

Conflict Resolution/Values: activities that look at values within the organizational context and at conflicts caused by differences between personal values and organizational values.

Consultation Skills: experiences that develop the skill of the internal or external consultant.

Facilitating Learning

Getting Acquainted: activities designed to "warm up" members of a learning group that is meeting for the first time.

Forming Subgroups: activities that help a newly formed learning group break into subgroups for learning purposes.

Expectations of Learners/Facilitators: activities for use when a gap potentially exists between what the learners expect and what the facilitator is offering.

Dealing with Blocks to Learning: activities developed to deal with situations in which learning is blocked through the interference of other dynamics, conscious or unconscious, in the group.

Building Trust: activities to create trust and a climate of openness and learning within the group.

Building Norms of Openness: activities that help group participants to expand their learning by being willing to give and receive feedback.

Energizers: activities that "recharge" the group when energy is low.

Evaluating Learning-Group Process: activities to help individuals evaluate what is taking place within a learning group.

Developing Group Facilitator Skills: activities designed to develop the abilities of trainers, group leaders, or group facilitators.

Closure: activities to use at the end of a training event.

Classifying these materials is somewhat arbitrary, because they can be adapted for a variety of training purposes. Although any given experience could belong to a number of classifications, we have listed each only once, categorizing it in the area of its *most probable* use.

PERSONAL

Self-Disclosure

Number	Title [Author]	Goals	Time Required	Volume & Page No.
16	**Fantasies:** Suggestions for Individuals and Groups	To promote heightened awareness of self and others.	Varies with each fantasy	I-75
20	**Graphics:** Self-Disclosure Activities	To generate self-disclosure data through graphics.	Varies with each activity	I-88
349	**Personality Traits:** Self-Discovery and Disclosure [W.J. Schiller]	To assist the participants in gaining insight about themselves. To facilitate self-disclosure.	Approximately one hour	IX-58
353	**Management Skills:** Assessing Personal Performance [C.J. Levin]	To heighten the participants' awareness of the wide range of behaviors that are encompassed by management.	One hour and twenty-five minutes	IX-93

Sensory

Number	Title [Author]	Goals	Time Required	Volume & Page No.
19	**Awareness Expansion:** A Potpourri	To heighten one's sensory awareness.	Varies with each activity	I-86
71	**Lemons:** A Sensory-Awareness Activity	To increase sensory awareness.	One hour	III-94
136	**Relaxation and Perceptual Awareness:** A Workshop [J.L. Hipple, M. Hutchins, & J. Barott]	To learn basic techniques of physical relaxation, breathing processes, and self-awareness. To experience one's physical state of existence and personal perceptions of inner and outer reality and fantasy.	Three hours	'74-84

Sensory (Continued)

Number	Title [Author]	Goals	Time Required	Volume & Page No.
199	**T'ai Chi Chuan:** An Introduction to Movement Awareness [D.X. Swenson]	To increase body self-awareness. To develop integrated, relaxed, economical, and balanced movement and activity. To facilitate a feeling of "centeredness" in the here-and-now.	Approximately one hour	VI-10

Feelings Awareness

Number	Title [Author]	Goals	Time Required	Volume & Page No.
56	**Feelings and Defenses:** A Spontaneous Lecture	To study feelings significant to group members and defenses they use. To help group members take responsibility for their own learning.	About thirty minutes	III-31
65	**Think-Feel:** A Verbal Progression [J.E. Jones]	To make distinctions between thoughts and feelings. To learn to link feeling feedback to observable behavior. To practice empathizing.	Forty-five minutes	III-70
75	**Frustrations and Tensions**	To help participants to become aware of their responses to tense, frustrating situations. To study alternative responses to such situations.	Approximately forty-five minutes	'72-5
119	**Group Exploration:** A Guided Fantasy [L. Berman]	To allow individuals to share their means of coping with fear and stress as well as their personal responses to pleasure.	Approximately one hour	IV-92

Feelings Awareness (Continued)

Number	Title [Author]	Goals	Time Required	Volume & Page No.
122	**Expressing Anger:** A Self-Disclosure Exercise [G.R. Gemmill]	To study styles of expressing anger in a group setting. To study effects of anger in a group setting. To legitimize the presence and expression of anger within groups. To identify behaviors which elicit anger in others. To explore ways of coping with anger.	Approximately forty-five minutes	IV-104
300	**Projections:** Interpersonal Awareness Expansion [B. Nisenholz]	To help participants to explore the process of projection. To provide an opportunity for participants to recognize how and what they project about others. To enable participants to become more aware of the part they play in the outcome of unpleasant situations.	One and one-half hours	VIII-30
330	**Feelings:** Verbal and Nonverbal Congruence [S.L. Norman]	To provide an opportunity to compare verbal and nonverbal components of feelings. To develop awareness of the congruence between verbal and nonverbal components of feelings. To increase sensitivity to the feelings of others.	One to one and one-half hours	'83-14
473	**Affirmations:** Positive Self-Talk [M.K. Prokop]	To understand the nature and purpose of affirmations. To offer members of an intact work group the opportunity to practice developing and using affirmations.	Approximately one hour	'91-9

Feelings Awareness (Continued)

Number	Title [Author]	Goals	Time Required	Volume & Page No.
485	**Coping Strategies:** Managing Stress Successfully [A.M. Gregory]	To offer the participants an opportunity to identify their own patterns of response to stressful situations. To assist the participants in identifying thoughts, feelings, and behaviors that help and hinder in coping with stress. To encourage the participants to generate alternatives for reducing their self-defeating reactions to stress and for enhancing the positive reactions that lead to successful outcomes.	Approximately one and one-half hours	'92-9

Feedback

Number	Title [Author]	Goals	Time Required	Volume & Page No.
13	**Johari Window:** An Experience in Self-Disclosure and Feedback	To introduce the concept of the Johari Window. To permit participants to process data about themselves in terms of self-disclosure and feedback.	Approximately two hours	I-65
23	**Coins:** Symbolic Feedback [J.W. Pfeiffer]	To experiment with giving feedback symbolically. To share feelings involved with giving, receiving, and rejection.	Approximately one and one-half hours	I-104
58	**Peer Perceptions:** A Feedback Experience [J.E. Jones]	To let each group member know to what degree he is seen to be similar to each other member. To study feeling reactions to being considered "different." To help each member define the dimensions of human similarity and dissimilarity he believes are important.	Two to three hours	III-41

Feedback (Continued)

Number	Title [Author]	Goals	Time Required	Volume & Page No.
97	**Puzzlement:** A "Mild" Confrontation [R.R. Kurtz]	To help participants confront each other's behavior in helpful ways. To stimulate the amount of feedback given and received in a group. To share the feelings involved in giving and receiving feedback.	Approximately one and one-half hours	'73-30
99	**Analyzing and Increasing Open Behavior:** The Johari Window [P.G. Hanson]	To describe open and closed behavior in terms of the Johari Window. To identify facilitating and inhibiting forces which affect the exchange of feedback. To encourage the development of increased open behavior in the group through facilitated feedback.	Approximately two and one-half hours	'73-38
107	**The Portrait Game:** Individual Feedback [F. Maire]	To allow participants to receive a composite feedback picture from the members of their group as a departure from single-source individual feedback. To provide an opportunity for participants to compare their individual perceptions of how the group is experiencing their behavior with the reality of the group's experience.	A minimum of twenty minutes per participant	IV-24

Feedback (Continued)

Number	Title [Author]	Goals	Time Required	Volume & Page No.
123	**Stretching:** Identifying and Taking Risks [R.R. Kurtz]	To help participants become aware of interpersonal behavior which is risky for them. To increase participants' awareness of the relationship between risk-taking behavior and the attainment of personal growth goals. To encourage risk-taking behavior as a way of expanding participants' behavioral repertoire.	Approximately two hours	IV-107
146	**Payday:** A Closure Activity [R.L. Bunning]	To provide for self- and group evaluation of each participant's performance within the group. To allow each participant to compare his self-evaluation with the group's evaluation of him. To give participants experience in evaluating others in a constructive, concrete manner.	Approximately one hour	'75-54
168	**Adjectives:** Feedback [J.E. Jones]	To help participants clarify values that apply to human relationships. To establish the norms of soliciting and giving both positive and negative feedback.	Approximately one hour	V-114
170	**Person Perception:** Feedback [R.H. Dolliver]	To provide feedback to individual group members about how they are perceived by others. To help participants clarify what underlies their tendency to categorize other persons.	Approximately one hour	V-131

Feedback (Continued)

Number	Title [Author]	Goals	Time Required	Volume & Page No.
198	**Choose an Object:** A Getting-Acquainted Activity [D.L. Thompson]	To increase perception of oneself. To provide an opportunity to share personal perceptions. To provide an opportunity to receive feedback on perceived behavior.	Approximately two hours	VI-7
209	**Introspection:** Personal Evaluation and Feedback [D.L. Smith]	To provide an opportunity for participants to compare their self-assessments with those of others.	Approximately forty-five minutes	VI-57
216	**Affirmation of Trust:** A Feedback Activity [B.P. Holleran]	To increase understanding of physical, intellectual, and emotional trust. To explore how the trust level existing in the group affects the openness of discussion. To provide an opportunity for group members to give each other feedback on trust.	Approximately two hours	VI-110
225	**Cards:** Personal Feedback [J.R. Luthi]	To encourage the exchange of personal feedback. To provide a means for giving and receiving personal feedback.	Approximately two hours	'78-34
303	**Developing Trust:** A Leadership Skill [W.J. Bailey]	To examine some of the behaviors and personal qualities that affect the process of establishing trust in relationships. To analyze current behaviors and attitudes related to establishing trust in relationships. To increase awareness of how one is perceived by others in regard to behaviors that enhance the building of trust.	Approximately two hours	VIII-45

Feedback (Continued)

Number	Title [Author]	Goals	Time Required	Volume & Page No.
315	**Giving and Receiving Feedback:** Contracting for New Behavior [J.E. Jones]	To provide an opportunity for members of a personal-growth group to give and receive feedback on their in-group to give and receive feedback on their in-group behavior. To enable participants to set behavioral goals for the remainder of the group experience.	Approximately three hours	VIII-125
355	**Feedback:** Increasing Self-Perceptions [C.R. Mill]	To facilitate the process of giving and receiving feedback in a group. To help the participants to understand the feedback that they receive. To promote a process for exploring the participants' "hidden" characteristics.	Approximately two hours	IX-107
377	**Pin Spotter:** Practicing Positive Feedback [M.N. Mann]	To assist the participants in assessing their abilities to provide feedback. To offer the participants an opportunity to practice creating positive feed-back statements.	One hour and fifteen minutes	'85-11
389	**Aloha:** A Feedback Experience [T.H. Patten, Jr.]	To offer the participants an opportunity to give and receive feedback about their strengths and opportu-nities for improvement in interpersonal relations. To provide closure at the end of an experiential-learning event.	Approximately forty-five minutes	X-5

Feedback (Continued)

Number	Title [Author]	Goals	Time Required	Volume & Page No.
390	**I Am, Don't You Think?:** Zodiac Feedback [J.C. Bryant]	To assist the participants in gaining insight about themselves and about their fellow group members. To provide the participants with an opportunity to compare their self-perceptions with others' perceptions of them. To heighten the participants' awareness of the ways in which a variety of member characteristics can enrich a group.	Approximately two hours	X-8
391	**Two Bags Full:** Feedback About Managerial Characteristics [A.R. Carey]	To offer the participants an opportunity to provide one another with feedback about their managerial traits and behaviors. To help each participant to determine his or her strengths and avenues for growth as a manager. To assist each participant in developing a set of action steps for personal growth as a manager.	Two hours	X-22
425	**Performance Appraisal:** A Practice Session [J.E. Oliver]	To give participants an opportunity to create agenda for performance appraisals. To allow participants to experience the roles of supervisor, subordinate, and observer in a performance appraisal. To provide participants with an opportunity to give and receive feedback on performance-appraisal techniques.	Approximately two and one-half hours	'87-11

Feedback (Continued)

Number	Title [Author]	Goals	Time Required	Volume & Page No.
426	**Seeing Ourselves as Others See Us:** Using Video Equipment for Feedback [G.L. Talbot]	To enable participants to compare the images they have of themselves with the images they project. To increase feedback skills. To help participants understand how the differences in self-image and projected image influence interaction.	Approximately one hour plus an additional ten minutes for each speaker	'87-17
449	**The Art of Feedback:** Providing Constructive Information [S.C. Bushardt & A.R. Fowler, Jr.]	To develop the participants' understanding of how to give and receive feedback. To offer the participants an opportunity to practice giving and/or receiving feedback. To develop the participants' understanding of the impact of receiving feedback. To develop the participants' understanding of how the feedback process can help an individual or a work group to improve functioning.	Approximately two and one-half hours	'89-9

Assumptions

Number	Title [Author]	Goals	Time Required	Volume & Page No.
213	**Sherlock:** An Inference Activity [R. Roskin]	To increase awareness of how prejudices, assumptions, and self-concepts influence perceptions and decisions. To explore the relationship between observation, knowledge, and inference. To help participants become aware of their personal preconceptions and biases.	Approximately one and one-half hours	VI-92

Assumptions (Continued)

Number	Title [Author]	Goals	Time Required	Volume & Page No.
227	**Young/Old Woman:** A Perception Experiment [W.R. Mulford]	To focus on individual reactions to the same stimulus. To examine the effects of the immediate environment on an individual's perception.	Fifty minutes	'78-40
229	**Pygmalion:** Clarifying Personal Biases [R.L. Bunning]	To discover how pre-conceived ideas may influence collective and/or individual actions. To allow participants to assess their current behavior in terms of previous "script-ing" and social pressure.	Approximately forty-five minutes	'78-51
247	**Prejudice:** An Awareness-Expansion Activity [R. Raine]	To share feelings and ideas about prejudices in a non-threatening manner. To explore the validity of common prejudices.	One to one and one-half hours	VII-15
273	**Managerial Characteristics:** Exploring Stereotypes [A.K. Gulezian]	To increase awareness of masculine and feminine characteristics typically associated with effective managerial performance. To examine the male-manager stereotype and its implications for women in management. To provide an opportunity to examine self-perceptions relating to the concept of masculinity/femininity.	One and one-half to two hours	'80-31
292	**Data Survey:** Exploring Stereotypes [T.J. Mulhern & M.A. Parashkevov]	To discover how one makes judgments about others on the basis of age, race, sex, or ethnic stereotypes. To provide an opportunity to examine personal reactions to the issue of prejudice.	Approximately one and one-half hours	'81-57

Assumptions (Continued)

Number	Title [Author]	Goals	Time Required	Volume & Page No.
305	**Sexism in Advertisements:** Exploring Stereotypes [A.J. Burr, D.C.L. Griffith, D.B. Lyon, G.E. Philpot, G.N. Powell, & D.L. Sehring]	To become more aware of sex-role stereotyping in advertisements. To identify elements of advertisements that do or do not reflect sex-role stereotyping. To increase awareness of the effects of social conditioning.	Approximately one and one-half hours	VIII-58
331	**Manager's Dilemma:** Theory X and Theory Y [R. Glaser & C. Glaser]	To help participants to become aware of their own philosophies of human resource management. To introduce the concepts in McGregor's Theory X and Theory Y. To allow participants to compare and discuss alternative courses of action in a management situation.	Approximately two and one-half hours	'83-19
344	**All Iowans Are Naive:** Breaking Cultural Stereotypes [M. Maggio & N.A. Good]	To increase the participants' awareness of the stereotypes that they hold. To provide the participants with an opportunity to share their feelings about being the objects of stereotyping. To allow the participants to observe how others feel when they are negatively stereotyped.	Approximately two hours	IX-14

Assumptions (Continued)

Number	Title [Author]	Goals	Time Required	Volume & Page No.
392	**Water Jars:** Developing Creativity in Problem Solving [S. Chintamani]	To demonstrate the development of mental blocks in problem solving. To illustrate that the process of solving problems of a repetitive nature poses a threat to creativity. To allow the participants to investigate ways of breaking mental blocks and fostering creative problem solving.	Approximately forty-five minutes	X-26
413	**Getting To Know You:** Different Approaches, Different Perceptions [D.E. Whiteside]	To introduce group members to one another. To demonstrate that our perceptions of others and our interactions with them are influenced by the information we solicit from them.	One to one and one-half hours. (Larger groups will require more time.)	'86-11
427	**Doctor, Lawyer, Indian Chief:** Occupational Stereotypes [M.K. Craig]	To increase awareness of occupational stereotypes and of how they impact interpersonal relationships. To allow participants to discuss their feelings about occupational stereotyping.	Approximately two hours. (More than seven dyads require more time.)	'87-21
437	**The Problem with Men/Women Is. . . :** Sex-Role Assumptions [J.R. Farber]	To help the participants to identify their own and others' assumptions about role expectations for men and women. To explore attitudes and feelings that surface when the participants begin comparing their assumptions and role expectations. To allow the participants to experience arguing in favor of a point of view with which they personally disagree.	Approximately two hours	'88-9

Values Clarification

Number	Title [Author]	Goals	Time Required	Volume & Page No.
143	**Ideal Cards:** A Self-Disclosure Activity [B.P. Holleran]	To encourage interaction and self-disclosure about ideals. To reveal group members' priorities for their ideals.	Approximately one and one-half hours	'75-43
233	**Banners:** A Value-Clarification Activity [M.A. Graham]	To increase self-under-standing and self-awareness of values, goals, and individual potential. To provide a forum for the public expression of personal values, potentials, and goal-achievement standards. Toexamine how life values, potential, and goal achievement affect decisions concerning-personal needs and aspirations.	Two to three hours	'79-9
261	**Wants Bombardment:** A Psychosynthesis Activity [J.E. Jones]	To increase awareness of competing wants in one's life situation. To attempt to prioritize and/or synthesize one's wants.	Approximately one and one-half hours	VII-105
283	**Louisa's Problem:** Value Clarification [C.E. Amesley]	To provide practice in clarifying issues and identifying values without passing judgment. To develop awareness of some of the factors affecting one's own value judgments and those of others. To provide an opportunity to exchange various points of view on a highly emotional issue.	Approximately two hours	'81-13

Values Clarification (Continued)

Number	Title [Author]	Goals	Time Required	Volume & Page No.
298	**Lifeline:** A Value-Clarification Activity [S.H. Wyant]	To increase awareness of social influences on the formation of attitudes, beliefs, values, and perceptions. To examine personal development and growth in the context of political history, social movements, and popular culture. To share differing values and orientations.	One and one-half hours	VIII-21
321	**Introjection:** Identifying Significant Beliefs [B. Nisenholz]	To help participants to recognize the sources of their significant beliefs. To provide an opportunity for participants to identify their current personal reactions to their significant beliefs. To enable participants to reconsider which significant beliefs they would like to retain and which they would like to modify.	One to one and one-half hours	'82-29
357	**Group Sell:** Advertising Group Values [T.A. Flanagan]	To explore the participants' reasons for joining groups and the attractiveness of different types of groups. To examine issues concerning group loyalties and values about groups.	One and one-half to two hours	IX-114
361	**Values and Decisions:** Checking for Congruence [G. Akin]	To help the participants to clarify their personal values. To explore the relationship between the participants' values and their major life decisions. To identify factors that affect commitment to values in decision making.	One hour and forty-five minutes	IX-146

Values Clarification (Continued)

Number	Title [Author]	Goals	Time Required	Volume & Page No.
362	**The Promotion:** Value Clarification [J.L. Mills]	To provide an opportunity for the participants to practice identifying and clarifying values. To help the participants to become aware of some of the factors that affect their own value judgments as well as those of others.	Two hours and fifteen minutes	IX-152
393	**Work-Needs Assessment:** Achievement, Affiliation, and Power [P. Doyle]	To develop the participants' awareness of the individual needs that motivate people to behave in certain ways in the work place. To assist each participant in determining the needs that motivate him or her in the work place.	One and one-half hours	X-31
414	**Dropping Out:** Exploring Changes in Life Style [M.R. Lavery]	To explore attitudes about the phenomenon of "dropping out." To identify professional and personal constraints that could motivate a person to "drop out" in order to change his or her life style.	Two and one-half to three hours	'86-15
415	**Raising Elizabeth:** Socializing Occupational Choices [J. Mills]	To explore socialization factors that predispose (women's) occupational choices, aspirations, and successes. To put these socialization factors into a personal context.	Approximately two hours	'86-21

Values Clarification (Continued)

Number	Title [Author]	Goals	Time Required	Volume & Page No.
438	**Understanding the Need for Approval:** Toward Personal Autonomy [A. Johnson]	To help participants understand how the need for approval affects behavior. To help participants become aware of how they are externally directed. To introduce techniques for fostering self-actualization. To encourage participants to contract for internal control.	One and one-half to two hours	'88-21
450	**The Girl and the Sailor:** Value Clarification	To help participants clarify values. To develop participants' awareness of factors affecting their own value judgments and those of others. To demonstrate how values affect relationships and group decisions.	Approximately two hours	'89-17
461	**Pie in the Sky:** Exploring Life Values [J.A. Patten & T.H. Patten, Jr.]	To help participants examine life and career values. To help participants examine their values. To help participants explore consistency between expressed values and actions.	Approximately two hours	'90-9
462	**Life Raft:** Experiencing Values	To help participants examine values in a dramatic way. To help participants identify feelings that accompany values. To encourage participants to explore feelings of self-worth. To increase awareness of how values influence group decision making.	One and one-half to two hours	'90-17

Values Clarification (Continued)

Number	Title [Author]	Goals	Time Required	Volume & Page No.
463	**What's in It for Me?:** Clarifying Work Values [K. Kreis]	To help the participants to determine what needs they seek to fulfill through their work. To help the participants to determine what needs are presently fulfilled through their work and how. To provide the participants with the opportunity to discuss ways to improve the match between what they seek and what they get from their work.	Approximately one and one-half hours	'90-21

Life/Career Planning

Number	Title [Author]	Goals	Time Required	Volume & Page No.
46	**Life Planning:** A Programmed Approach	To apply concepts of planned change to an individual's personal, interpersonal, and career development.	Six hours split into thre two-hour periods	II-101
137	**What Do You See?:** A Discovery Activity [A.G. Kirn]	To expand awareness of these things that have meaning for life and work. work. To discover new areas of individual relevance and interest. To promote changing negative thinking to positive thinking.	A minimum of one hour	'75-7
332	**Career Renewal:** A Self-Inventory	To introduce the concept of job renewal. To enable participants to evaluate their present jobs in light of their stated career goals.	Approximately one hour	'83-27

Life/Career Planning (Continued)

Number	Title [Author]	Goals	Time Required	Volume & Page No.
363	**Training Philosophies:** A Personal Assessment [G.E.H. Beamish]	To assist the participants in clarifying their individual training philosophies. To help the participants to clarify their perceptions of the relationship between training and management.	One hour	IX-159
378	**Life Assessment and Planning:** Choosing the Future [A.J. Schuh]	To help each participant to review personal values and past experiences and to establish a plan for the future. To offer the participants an opportunity to experience peer feedback.	Approximately four hours	'85-15
394	**The Ego-Radius Model:** Evaluating and Planning Life Situations	To assist each participant in clarifying and evaluating his or her present life situation and in planning the life situation desired in the future.	Two hours	X-41
416	**Roles:** Understanding Sources of Stress [P. Doyle]	To enable participants to explore the diverse roles they are expected to fill. To help participants to understand the characteristics of these roles. To illustrate the potential for stress caused by the different expectations of diverse roles. To provide an opportunity for the participants to develop solutions to their own role conflicts.	Approximately two hours	'86-27

Life/Career Planning (Continued)

Number	Title [Author]	Goals	Time Required	Volume & Page No.
439	**Creating Ideal Personal Futures:** Using the Self-Fulfilling Prophecy [J.D. Adams]	To help the participants to develop awareness of the ways in which their non-conscious thought processes influence the results they achieve in life. To provide the participants with a technique for transforming inhibiting ways of thinking and behaving into ways of thinking and behaving that support the achievement of desired results. To help each participant to establish a sense of his or her purpose in life and to write a statement of this purpose.	Approximately one hour and fifty minutes	'88-31
486	**Supporting Cast:** Examining Personal Support Networks [M.K. Prokop]	To acquaint the participants with the characteristics of a supporting cast—the network of people who help a person to achieve his or her personal and professional goals. To offer the participants an opportunity to explore the roles that others play in their lives. To provide an opportunity for the participants to identify roles in their personal support networks that need to be filled or enhanced and to develop action plans to fill those needs.	Approximately two hours	'92-15

COMMUNICATION

Communication Awareness Experiments (Oral)

Number	Title [Author]	Goals	Time Required	Volume & Page No.
4	**One-Way, Two-Way:** A Communications Experiment [*adapted from* H.J. Leavitt]	To conceptualize the superior functioning of two-way communication through participatory demonstration. To examine the application of communication in family, social, and occupational settings.	Approximately forty-five minutes	I-13
28	**Rumor Clinic:** A Communications Experiment	To illustrate distortions which may occur in transmission of information from an original source through several individuals to a final destination.	Thirty minutes	II-12
108	**Ball Game:** Controlling and Influencing Communication [R.D. Jorgenson]	To explore the dynamics of assuming leadership in a group. To increase awareness of the power held by the member of a group who is speaking at any given time. To diagnose communication patterns in a group.	Approximately thirty minutes	IV-27
128	**Re-Owning:** Increasing Behavioral Alternatives [H.B. Karp]	To assist participants in exploring aspects of themselves that they might not be presently aware of or may be under-utilizing. To extend the range of behavioral alternatives open for effective communication.	Approximately one hour	'74-18

Communication Awareness Experiments (Oral) (Continued)

Number	Title [Author]	Goals	Time Required	Volume & Page No.
202	**Dominoes:** A Communication Experiment [S.H. Putnam]	To enhance awareness of factors that help or hinder effective interpersonal communication. To explore the effect on task-oriented behavior of shared versus unshared responsibility.	Approximately one and one-half hours	VI-21
241	**Blivet:** A Communication Experience [K. Myers, R. Tandon, & H. Bowens, Jr.]	To demonstrate and experience one-way and two-way verbal communication. To demonstrate and experience barriers and aids to verbal communication. To explore the effects of different status positions on interpersonal communication.	Approximately one and one-half hours	'79-46
250	**Meanings Are in People:** Perception Checking [J.N. Wismer]	To demonstrate that meanings are not in words but in the people who use them and hear them. To illustrate that our perceptions of words attribute positive, neutral, and negative meanings to them.	One to three hours	VII-28
251	**Mixed Messages:** A Communication Experiment [B.K. Holmberg & D.W. Mullene]	To explore the dynamics of receiving verbal and non-verbal communication cues that are in conflict with one another. To examine how nonverbal cues can convey listener attitudes that can affect the communication process. To develop an understanding of the importance and impact of being direct and congruent in all forms of interpersonal communication.	Approximately forty-five minutes to one hour	VII-34

Communication Awareness Experiments (Oral) (Continued)

Number	Title [Author]	Goals	Time Required	Volume & Page No.
307	**Maze:** One-Way and Two-Way Communication [G.L. Talbot]	To experience the effects of free versus restricted communication in accomplishing a task. To explore the impact of communication processes on the development of trust between a leader and a follower.	Approximately one and one-half to two hours	VIII-64
309	**Resistance:** A Role Play [H.B. Karp]	To provide an opportunity to experience the effects of two different approaches to dealing with resistance. To increase awareness of typical responses to attempts to break down resistance. To develop strategies for coping with resistance from others.	Two to two and one-half hours	VIII-75
310	**Organizational TA:** Interpersonal Communication [R. Strand & F.R. Wickert]	To gain insight into the effects on communication of the three ego states. parent (P), adult (A), and child (C). To have the experience of operating from each of these three ego stages in confrontation situations. To acquire skills in observing interactions based on these three ego states. To explore the benefits of operating from an adult ego state in confrontation situations.	Approximately two hours	VIII-83

Communication Awareness Experiments (Oral) (Continued)

Number	Title [Author]	Goals	Time Required	Volume & Page No.
341	**Synonyms:** Sharing Perceptions Between Groups [P. Leamon]	To offer two different groups an opportunity to compare the ways in which they perceive and talk about their worlds. To illustrate that people's language both expands and limits their worlds. To improve understanding between two groups.	Approximately one hour	IX-5
395	**I'm All Ears:** Enhancing Awareness of Effective Listening [J.I. Costigan & S.K. Tyson]	To develop the participants' awareness of some of the requirements for listening effectively. To explore the effects of distractions on a person's ability to listen.	One hour and forty-five minutes	X-46
396	**In Other Words:** Building Oral-Communication Skills	To acquaint the participants with some useful tips regarding effective oral communication. To allow the participants to practice translating long, written messages into short but accurate and effective oral ones. To offer the participants an opportunity to give and receive feedback about the effectiveness of their translations and their delivery.	Approximately one and one-half hours	X-55
397	**Taking Responsibility:** Practice in Communicating Assumptions [G.L. Talbot]	To develop the participants' understanding of the effects of assumptions on oral communication. To offer the participants an opportunity to practice devising comments that demonstrate their willingness to assume responsibility for stating their assumptions.	Two hours	X-62

Communication Awareness Experiments (Oral) (Continued)

Number	Title [Author]	Goals	Time Required	Volume & Page No.
398	**Pass It On:** Simulating Organizational Communication [L.C. Lederman & L.P. Stewart]	To enhance the participants' understanding of the complexity of oral communication patterns within an organization. To illustrate what happens to messages that are transmitted orally through several different channels within an organization. To explore ways to improve oral communication within an organization.	One hour and forty-five minutes	X-68
440	**E-Prime:** Distinguishing Facts from Opinions [G.L. Talbot]	To foster the participants' awareness of how they speak about others and how they interpret comments about others. To assist the participants in distinguishing definitive from associative attributes (facts from opinions) used in conversation.	Approximately one hour and five minutes	'88-39
441	**VMX Productions, Inc:** Handling Résistance Positively [H.B. Karp]	To increase the participants' understanding of resistance. To provide an opportunity for the participants to explore and compare strategies for dealing with resistance. To present the participants with a positive and effective method for handling resistance.	One hour and twenty minutes to one and one-half hours	'88-43

Communication Awareness Experiments (Oral) (Continued)

Number	Title [Author]	Goals	Time Required	Volume & Page No.
464	**Words Apart:** Bridging the Communication Gap [M. Maier]	To help the participants to become aware of gender influences on conversation style. To provide the participants with the opportunity to experience artificial restrictions on their conversational styles. To help the participants to become aware of conversational patterns and styles.	One hour	'90-29
465	**In Reply:** Responding to Feeling Statements [H.F. Sweitzer & M.A. Kosh]	To offer the participants an opportunity to experience the positive and negative effects that various ways of responding to statements of feelings can have on the sender and the recipient. To help the participants to identify their usual patterns of sending and receiving responses to feeling statements and ways in which they might want to alter these patterns. To help the participants to identify the responses to statements of feelings that are beneficial to continuing communication.	Approximately three hours	'90-35
474	**Supportive Versus Defensive Climates:** How Would You Say. . . ? [J.C.B. Teboul]	To acquaint participants with six supportive and six defensive communication dimensions. To develop participants' abilities to recognize supportive and defensive communication. To provide participants with an opportunity to create messages that foster supportive and defensive climates.	One hour and twenty minutes	'91-15

Communication Awareness Experiments (Oral) (Continued)

Number	Title [Author]	Goals	Time Required	Volume & Page No.
475	**Quality Customer Service:** When the Going Gets Tough [B. Jameson]	To increase the participants' understanding of customer behaviors. To enhance the participants' awareness of their own responses to customer behaviors. To offer the participants an opportunity to share ideas about dealing with difficult customers. To help the participants to identify the behaviors that create a positive relationship with customers.	One and one-half to two hours	'91-27
476	**The Parking Space:** Relationships and Negotiating [L. Porter & F.F. Jandt]	To develop the participants' understanding of the effects of relationships on negotiations. To help the participants to become more aware of how changes in roles affect negotiations. To help the participants to develop negotiation skills.	One and one-half hours	'91-35
487	**Feedback Awareness:** Skill Building for Supervisors [R.W. Lucas]	To enhance the participants' awareness of the impact of feedback. To offer principles and guidelines for giving and receiving feedback. To provide a vehicle for practice in giving and receiving feedback. To offer the participants an opportunity to discuss and identify feedback characteristics and techniques.	Two hours to two hours and fifteen minutes	'92-29

Communication Awareness Experiments (Nonverbal)

Number	Title [Author]	Goals	Time Required	Volume & Page No.
22	**Nonverbal Communication:** A Collection of Activities	To learn new ways of expressing one's feelings, independent of one's vocabulary. To express feelings authentically using nonverbal symbolism. To focus on nonverbal cues that one emits.	Varies with each activity	I-101
44	**Nonverbal Communication:** A Collection	To learn new ways of expressing one's feelings, independent of one's vocabulary. To express feelings authentically using nonverbal symbolism. To focus on nonverbal cues that one emits.	Varies with each activity	II-94
50	**Behavior Description Triads:** Reading Body Language	To practice describing nonverbal behavior objectively, without interpretation. To study the body-language messages that accompany verbalization. To alert group members to the variety of signals they use to communicate.	Approximately fifteen minutes	I-6
72	**Nonverbal Communication:** A Collection	To learn new ways of expressing one's feelings, independent of one's vocabulary. To express feelings authentically using nonverbal symbolism. To focus on nonverbal cues that one emits.	Varies with each activity	III-97

Communication Awareness Experiments (Nonverbal) (Continued)

Number	Title [Author]	Goals	Time Required	Volume & Page No.
286	**Gestures:** Perceptions and Responses [S.L. Norman]	To provide an opportunity for participants to examine the perceptual biases operating in their interpretation of gestures. To increase awareness of the ambiguity inherent in various forms of nonverbal communication. To demonstrate how one gesture can elicit different feeling responses among different persons. To examine the principle that verbal and nonverbal communication must be congruent to be effective.	Approximately one and one-half hours	'81-28

Communication Awareness Experiments (Oral/Nonverbal)

Number	Title [Author]	Goals	Time Required	Volume & Page No.
153	**Babel:** Interpersonal Communication [P.M. Ericson]	To examine language barriers which contribute to breakdown in communication. To demonstrate the anxieties and frustrations that may be felt when communicating under difficult circumstances. To illustrate the impact of nonverbal communication when verbal communication is ineffective and/or restricted.	Approximately two hours	V-16
175	**Blindfolds:** A Dyadic Experience [J.I. Costigan & A.L. Dirks]	To demonstrate and experience the need for visual cues in perception and communication. To demonstrate the need for visual cues in the definition of "personal space."	Approximately one hour	'76-13

Communication Awareness Experiments (Oral/Nonverbal) (Continued)

Number	Title [Author]	Goals	Time Required	Volume & Page No.
379	**Feedback on Nonverbal and Verbal Behaviors:** Building Communication Awareness [G.L. Talbot]	To enhance the participants' awareness of their own and others' nonverbal and verbal communication patterns. To offer the participants an opportunity to give and receive feedback about their communication patterns.	Approximately two hours and forty-five minutes	'85-35
417	**Shades of Difference:** Exploring Metaverbal Communication [A.C. Ballew]	To demonstrate the impact that metaverbal aspects of communication have on the perception and interpretation of meaning. To allow the participants to practice using metaverbal aspects of communication.	Approximately two and one-half hours	'86-35

Developing Interpersonal Trust in Dyads

Number	Title [Author]	Goals	Time Required	Volume & Page No.
21	**Dyadic Encounter:** A Program for Developing Relationships [J.E. Jones & J.J. Jones]	To explore knowing and trusting another person through mutual self-disclosure and risk taking.	A minimum of two hours	I-90
70	**Intimacy Program:** Developing Personal Relationships [*adapted from S.M. Jourard*]	To accelerate the getting acquainted process in groups. To study the experience of self-disclosure. To develop authenticity in groups.	Approximately one and one-half hours	III-89

Developing Interpersonal Trust in Dyads (Continued)

Number	Title [Author]	Goals	Time Required	Volume & Page No.
116	**Dialog:** A Program for Developing Work Relationships [J.E. Jones & J.J. Jones]	To increase openness in work relationships. To generate higher trust in interpersonal relations in work settings. To clarify assumptions that persons who work together make about each other and each other's jobs.	A minimum of two hours	IV-66
138	**Party Conversations:** A FIRO Role-Play [C.L. Kormanski]	To experiment with different types of interpersonal behavior. To demonstrate the concepts in Schutz's theory of interpersonal relations.	Approximately two and one-half hours	'75-10
169	**Dyadic Renewal:** A Program for Developing Ongoing Relationships [C.A. Kelley & J.S. Colladay]	To periodically explore various aspects of a relationship through mutual self-disclosure and risk taking.	A minimum of two hours	V-116
180	**Disclosing and Predicting:** A Perception-Checking Activity [J. Lalanne]	To aid participants in developing social perception skills. To familiarize participants with the concept of accurate empathy. To demonstrate the effects that first impressions can have on perceptions.	Approximately thirty minutes	'76-46
190	**Letter Exchange:** A Dyadic Focus on Feelings [A.G. Kirn]	To provide a practical, low-threat, repeatable framework for sharing feelings as a step toward building a dyadic relationship. To promote self-disclosure and interpersonal risk taking.	Approximately one hour	'77-28

Developing Interpersonal Trust in Dyads (Continued)

Number	Title [Author]	Goals	Time Required	Volume & Page No.
220	**Dyadic Risk Taking:** A Perception Check [K.G. Albrecht & W.C. Boshear]	To experience the feelings associated with mild risk-taking behavior. To experiment with controlling the level of risk one is willing to take. To experience specific feedback on the degree to which another perceives one's risk.	Approximately one hour	VI-130
242	**Conflict Management:** Dyadic Sharing [M. Robert]	To identify and share reactions to ways of dealing with conflict. To explore new ideas about managing conflict.	Approximately one hour	'79-54
262	**Physical Characteristics:** Dyadic Perception Checking [A.J. Schuh]	To examine one's reactions to the physical characteristics of others. To learn to observe others more accurately. To study the effects of generalizing and stereotyping.	Forty-five minutes to one hour	VII-108

Sexual Awareness

Number	Title [Author]	Goals	Time Required	Volume & Page No.
226	**Sexual Assessment:** Self-Disclosure [P.S. Weikert]	To share sexual perceptions, feelings, attitudes, values, behaviors, and expectations. To clarify one's sexuality through self-disclosure. To gain insight into the sexual dimensions of other persons.	Approximately two and one-half hours	'78-36

Sexual Awareness (Continued)

Number	Title [Author]	Goals	Time Required	Volume & Page No.
249	**Sexual Values:** Relationship Clarification [P.S. Weikert]	To identify one's own values about a sexual relationship. To become aware of the sexual values of others. To increase awareness of the many components of sexual relationships.	One and one-half hours	VII-24
272	**Sexual Attraction:** A Written Role Play [J.B. Driscoll & R.A. Bova]	To explore the dynamics of sexual attraction among co-workers. To heighten awareness of the effect that assumptions can have on the shaping of an evolving relationship. To provide an opportunity for participants to explore their personal interpretations of, assumptions about, and responses to issues regarding sexual attraction.	Approximately one hour and forty-five minutes	'80-26
466	**Tina Carlan:** Resolving Sexual Harassment in the Workplace [J.A. Sample]	To develop the participants' awareness of legal issues in connection with sexual harassment complaints. To provide the participants with a systematic process for investigating and resolving sexual harassment within an organization. To provide the participants with a group learning forum for how to resolve sexual harassment in the workplace. To provide an opportunity to examine personal reactions to the issue of sexual harassment.	Approximately three hours and fifteen minutes	'90-45

Listening

Number	Title [Author]	Goals	Time Required	Volume & Page No.
8	**Listening Triads:** Building Communications Skills	To develop skills in active listening. To study barriers to effective listening.	Approximately forty-five minutes	I-31
52	**Not-Listening:** A Dyadic Role-Play [H.B. Karp]	To allow participants to experience the frustration of not being heard. To promote listening readiness.	Approximately thirty minutes	III-10
152	**Helping Relationships:** Verbal and Nonverbal Communication [C.G. Carney]	To demonstrate the effects of posturing and eye contact on helping relationships. To focus group members' attention on the impact of their non-verbal behaviors on other individuals. To teach basic nonverbal listening and attending skills.	Approximately thirty minutes	V-13
238	**Defensive and Supportive Communication:** A Dyadic Role Play [G.W. Combs]	To examine the dynamics of defensive and supportive communi-cation in supervisor/ subordinate relationships. To develop skills in listening to and under-standing a contrasting point of view. To explore the concept of synergy in dyadic communication. To examine the expecta-tions that defensive com-munication creates for a continuing relationship.	Approximately one and one-half hours	'79-28
252	**Active Listening:** A Communication Skills Practice [J.N. Wismer]	To identify the emotional messages that are often hidden in communication. To gain practice in active-listening skills.	Approximately one and one-half hours	VII-39

Listening (Continued)

Number	Title [Author]	Goals	Time Required	Volume & Page No.
257	**Sunglow:** An Appraisal Role Play [J.M. Rigby]	To practice skills in counseling, coaching, and active listening. To increase awareness of behavioral and interpersonal factors that influence an interview. To provide feedback on interviewing effectiveness.	Two to two and one-half hours	VII-73
428	**Poor Listening Habits:** Identifying and Improving Them [J. Seltzer & L.W. Howe]	To help participants to identify their poor listening habits. To allow participants to practice effective listening skills.	Approximately one and one-half hours	'87-25

Interviewing

Number	Title [Author]	Goals	Time Required	Volume & Page No.
142	**Live Case:** A Group Diagnosis [R.K. Conyne & D.H. Frey]	To illustrate problems involved in overgeneralizing. To practice interviewing techniques as a method of generating data about an individual. To study the process of forming hypotheses from available information.	Approximately two hours	'75-40
333	**Assistant Wanted:** An Employment Interview [L.M. Graves & C.A. Lowe]	To provide participants with an experience in interviewing and in being interviewed. To explore the dynamics of the interviewer-interviewee relationship. To introduce the components of the employment interview.	Approximately two to two and one-half hours	'83-31

Interviewing (Continued)

Number	Title [Author]	Goals	Time Required	Volume & Page No.
358	**Interviewing:** Gathering Pertinent Information [K.L. Murrell]	To help the participants to become familiar with the interviewing process from the interviewer's perspective. To allow the participants to practice developing criteria that a job candidate must meet based on the nature and duties of the job. To assist the participants in developing ways to elicit pertinent information from job candidates.	One hour and forty-five minutes	IX-122
365	**Inquiries and Discoveries:** Managing Interviewing Situations [E. Solender]	To identify effective and ineffective interviewing techniques. To help the participants to develop skills in conducting interviews with different types of respondents.	One and one-half to two hours	'84-9
451	**What's Legal?:** Investigating Employment Interview Questions [R.J. Cantwell]	To develop the participants' awareness of legal issues in connection with interviewing applicants for employment. To assist the participants in identifying legal and illegal employment-interview questions and in determining why they are legal or illegal. To give the participants an opportunity to practice devising legal employment-interview questions.	Approximately two hours and forty-five minutes	'89-23

Assertion

Number	Title [Author]	Goals	Time Required	Volume & Page No.
130	**Conflict Fantasy:** A Self-Examination [J.A. Stepsis]	To facilitate awareness of strategies for dealing with conflict situations. To examine methods of responding to conflict. To introduce the strategy of negotiation and to present the skills required for successful negotiation.	Approximately forty-five minutes	'74-22
181	**Boasting:** A Self Enhancement Activity [J.J. Rosenblum & J.E. Jones]	To help participants identify, own, and share their personal strengths. To explore feelings and reactions to sharing "boasts" with other participants. To experience the enhanced sense of personal power in announcing one's strengths to others.	Approximately one hour and fifteen minutes	'76-49
206	**Submission/ Aggression/Assertion:** Nonverbal Components [G.N. Weiskott & M.E. Sparks]	To experience and differentiate the nonverbal components of assertive behavior from those of aggressive and submissive (nonassertive) behavior. To increase awareness of one's own assertive behavior.	Approximately thirty minutes to one hour	VI-36
219	**Escalation:** An Assertion Activity [C. Kelley]	To allow participants to experience success in communicating while under stress. To enable participants to practice communicating effectively in stressful situations.	One to two hours	VI-127

Assertion (Continued)

Number	Title [Author]	Goals	Time Required	Volume & Page No.
306	**Praise:** Giving and Receiving Positive Feedback [T.J. Mason]	To develop an awareness of one's own accomplishments. To practice giving public recognition to others. To become aware of one's responses to recognition from others.	One and one-half to two hours	VIII-61
380	**Gaining Support:** Four Approaches [J. Spoth, B.H. Morris, & T.C. Denton]	To acquaint the participants with various approaches to developing individual support within a group. To develop the participants' awareness of the positive and negative consequences of these approaches.	Approximately two hours	'85-39
399	**The Human Bank Account:** Practicing Self-Affirmation	To increase the participants' awareness of their own and others' ability to affect their self-concepts. To offer the participants an opportunity to practice assuming control of their self-concepts and making self-affirming responses to comments made by others.	Two hours	X-76
400	**The Decent but Pesky Co-Worker:** Developing Contracting Skills [L. Porter]	To acquaint the participants with the significance and usefulness of contracting as a means of facilitating the helping process. To develop the participants' understanding of and skills in contracting.	Approximately one and one-half hours	X-80

GROUP CHARACTERISTICS

Process Observation/Awareness

Number	Title [Author]	Goals	Time Required	Volume & Page No.
6	**Group-On-Group:** A Feedback Experience	To develop skills in process observation. To develop skills in giving appropriate feedback to individual group members.	Approximately one hour	I-22
9	**Committee Meeting:** Demonstrating Hidden Agendas [*based on J. Gold & L. Miller*]	To illustrate the effects of hidden agendas on task accomplishment in a work group.	Approximately one and one-half hours	I-36
10	**Process Observation:** A Guide	To provide feedback to a group concerning its process. To provide experience for group members in observing process variables in group meetings.	Minimum of ten minutes for processing	I-45
29	**Group Tasks:** A Collection of Activities	To be used in studying group process.	Varies with each activity	II-16
37	**Self-Interaction-Task:** Process Observation Guides [J.E. Jones]	To practice observing small-group process. To gain experience in reporting process observations to a group. To provide instrumental feedback on one's interpersonal orientations.	Two hours	II-68
39	**Group Development:** A Graphic Analysis [J.E. Jones]	To compare the development of a small group along the dimensions of task functions and personal relations. To compare members' perceptions of the developmental status of a group at a given time.	Approximately forty-five minutes	II-76
79	**What To Look for in Groups:** An Observation Guide [P.G. Hanson]	To assist group members in understanding and being more perceptive about group process.	Three hours	'72-19

Process Observation/Awareness (Continued)

Number	Title [Author]	Goals	Time Required	Volume & Page No.
124	**The In-Group:** Dynamics of Exclusion [G. Goldberg]	To allow participants to experience consciously excluding and being excluded. To confront feelings which exclusion generates. To examine processes by which social identity is conferred by the excluding group and accepted by the excluded member.	Approximately one and one-half hours	IV-112
126	**Cog's Ladder:** A Process-Observation Activity [G.O. Charrier]	To enhance awareness of factors which distinguish process from content in group interaction. To explore a model of group development.	One hour	'74-8
208	**Team Development:** A TORI Model [G.R. Gemmill]	To study TORI growth processes. To practice applying a theoretical model to group self-diagnosis.	Approximately two and one-half hours	VI-54
254	**Stones, Bands, and Circles:** Sociogram Activities [D.E. Miskiman; J.E. Hoover & M.A. Goldstein; D. Anderson]	To explore existing levels of interaction, influence, and inclusion in a group. To develop an awareness of group dynamics.	Approximately forty-five minutes to one hour per activity	VII-53
270	**Baseball Game:** Group Membership Functions [R.W. Rasberry]	To gain insight into how one is perceived by others. To study the variety of functions performed by group members. To introduce a novel way of characterizing group-member roles.	Approximately three hours	'80-14

Process Observation/Awareness (Continued)

Number	Title [Author]	Goals	Time Required	Volume & Page No.
276	**Slogans:** A Group-Development Activity [S.M. Sant]	To experience the processes and feelings that arise when a new member joins an ongoing group with defined tasks and roles. To explore the coping mechanisms adopted by the individual and the group to deal with entry problems. To examine functional and dysfunctional coping strategies of groups.	Approximately three hours	'80-51
299	**Group Identity:** A Developmental Planning Session [K.W. Howard]	To provide the members of an intact group with a model for understanding the factors that influence its development. To enable the members of an intact group to identify its current stage of growth. To promote group cohesiveness by exploring the needs and interests of its members.	Approximately two hours	VIII-25
366	**The Seven Pieces:** Identifying Group Roles [N.J. Carpenter]	To introduce the participants to the roles that emerge in a group. To provide the participants with an opportunity to experience and assume some of these roles and to observe their impact on the group process.	Approximately one hour	'84-16
367	**MACE:** Demonstrating Factors That Affect Performance [S. Dakin & R.Robb]	To demonstrate that individual performance within a group is influenced by four major factors: *motivation, ability, conditions, and expectations* (MACE).	One to one and one-half hours	'84-22

Process Observation/Awareness (Continued)

Number	Title [Author]	Goals	Time Required	Volume & Page No.
418	**Group Sociogram II:** Perceptions of Interaction [A.C. Ballew]	To help the members of an intact group to express their perceptions of and feelings about the relationships within the group. To identify existing patterns of interaction within an intact group. To encourage communication and the sharing of perceptions within the group. To "open up" an intact group for team-building efforts.	Approximately two and one-half hours	'86-41
429	**Ranking Characteristics:** A Comparison of Decision-Making Approaches [C.A. LaJeunesse]	To allow participants to experience three types of decision-making processes: autocratic, democratic, and consensual. To demonstrate and compare the relative time required for each of these processes. To explore the impacts of each of these approaches on the quality of the decisions, the participants' degree of involvement in the processes, and their preferences for a particular approach.	One to one and one-half hours	'87-31

Leadership-Membership/Power

Number	Title [Author]	Goals	Time Required	Volume & Page No.
59	**Line-Up and Power Inversion:** An Experiment	To expand the individual's awareness of his influence on the group. To experience power inversion.	Approximately one and one-half hours	III-46

Leadership-Membership/Power (Continued)

Number	Title [Author]	Goals	Time Required	Volume & Page No.
121	**Toothpicks:** An Analysis of Helping Behaviors [R.R. Middleman]	To identify differing approaches to assisting others in a task. To explore the effects of the various helping approaches on task accomplishment and interpersonal relations.	Approximately one hour	IV-99
167	**Cups:** A Power Experience [A.J. Reilly]	To increase awareness of the meanings of power. To experience giving, receiving, and not receiving power.	Approximately two hours	V-111
266	**Power Personalities:** An OD Role Play [L.A. Jean, J.R. Pilgrim, G.N. Powell, D.K. Stoltz, & O.S. White]	To provide an opportunity to practice various power styles and behaviors. To learn which powerseeking tactics and bases of power are effective or ineffective in a problem-solving situation. To examine individual perceptions of and reactions to various power strategies.	Approximately one and one-half to two hours	VII-127
277	**Power and Affiliation:** A Role Play [J.F. Veiga & J.N. Yanouzas]	To become better acquainted with positive and negative aspects of power and affiliation. To explore the dynamics of power and affiliation in managerial situations.	Approximately one hour and forty-five minutes	'80-54
346	**Power Caucus:** Defining and Negotiating [B.F. Spencer]	To help the participants to clarify their own definitions of power. To allow the participants to experience the similarities and differences between these definitions and the application of power in a real situation.	One hour and forty-five minutes	IX-31

Leadership-Membership/Power (Continued)

Number	Title [Author]	Goals	Time Required	Volume & Page No.
368	**Role Power:** Understanding Influence [P.E. Doyle]	To explore the types of power inherent in different roles in group settings. To acquaint the participants with various power strategies that can be used in a decision-making process. To help the participants to develop an understanding of effective and ineffective uses of power.	Approximately two hours	'84-26
401	**Choose Me:** Developing Power Within a Group [L. Porter]	To explore issues related to power and influence within a group. To offer each participant an opportunity to influence the other members of his or her group. To allow the participants to give and receive feedback about their personal approaches to developing power and influence within a group.	Approximately two hours and fifteen minutes	X-85
402	**Power and Affection Exchange:** Sharing Feelings [G.J. Rath]	To offer the participants an opportunity to express their feelings for one another. To explore the participants' feelings about power and affection.	Approximately two hours	X-88

Leadership-Membership/Power (Continued)

Number	Title [Author]	Goals	Time Required	Volume & Page No.
477	**Bases of Power:** Developing the Group's Potential [M.H. Kitzmiller]	To acquaint the participants with the different bases of power. To assist the participants in identifying the power bases resident in their group and how those forms of power affect the group. To assist the participants in recognizing their own potential for developing and using power. To assist each participant in creating an action plan for enhancing his or her power bases.	Approximately three to three and one-half hours for a group with six members. A group with more than six members may require considerably more time	'91-43

Leadership-Membership/Styles

Number	Title [Author]	Goals	Time Required	Volume & Page No.
3	**T-P Leadership Questionnaire:** An Assessment of Style *[adapted from Sergiovanni, Metzcus, & Burden]*	To evaluate oneself in terms of task orientation and people orientation.	Approximately forty-five minutes	I-7
154	**Styles of Leadership:** A Series of Role Plays [G.M. Phillips]	To explore the impact that leaders have on decision making groups. To demonstrate the effects of hidden agendas.	Approximately two hours	V-19
162	**Pins and Straws:** Leadership Styles [H.L. Fromkin]	To dramatize three general styles of leadership: autocratic, laissez-faire, and democratic. To increase awareness of how different styles of leadership can affect the performance of subordinates. To study the phenomenon of competition among groups.	Approximately two hours	V-78

Leadership-Membership/Styles (Continued)

Number	Title [Author]	Goals	Time Required	Volume & Page No.
207	**Staff Meeting:** A Leadership Role Play [E.M. Schuttenberg]	To illustrate various styles of leadership and patterns of accommodation. To explore the effects of the interaction of leadership style and pattern of accommodation on individual motivation and decision making.	Approximately two and one-half hours. Additional time is required if lecturettes are to be presented	VI-39
274	**Choosing an Apartment:** Authority Issues in Groups [J.J. Szucko, R.L. Greenblatt, & C.B. Keys]	To experience the impact of authoritarian behavior during a competitive activity. To increase personal awareness of reactions to authoritarian behavior. To experience the effects of hidden agendas on decision making processes.	Two hours	'80-37
296	**Boss Wanted:** Identifying Leadership Characteristics [G.L. Williams]	To allow individuals to examine their personal criteria for a good manager. To compare preferences about managerial qualities. To increase awareness of one's own current managerial strengths and weaknesses.	Approximately one and one-half hours	VIII-15
369	**Follow the Leader:** An Introduction to Situational Leadership™ [K.S. Brown & D.M. Loppnow]	To allow the participants to experience each of the four leadership styles that constitute the basis of Situational Leadership™ theory. To explore the ways in which leadership styles, tasks, and work groups affect one another.	Approximately two and one-half hours	'84-38

Leadership-Membership/Styles (Continued)

Number	Title [Author]	Goals	Time Required	Volume & Page No.
381	**Management Perspectives:** Identifying Styles [P. Doyle]	To help the participants to identify various managerial styles. To illustrate the ways in which these managerial styles can affect an organization. To acquaint participants with the advantages and disadvantages of these styles.	Two hours and fifteen minutes	'85-45
452	**Four Factors:** The Influence of Leader Behavior [W.N. Parker]	To acquaint the participants with Rosenthal and Jacobson's (1968) four-factor theory explaining a leader's influence on followers and the effect of this influence on follower behavior. To give the participants an opportunity to analyze case studies showing how particular leader approaches to Rosenthal and Jacobson's four factors (climate, feedback, input, and output) can positively or negatively affect followers.	Approximately one hour and forty-five minutes	'89-39
478	**Rhetoric and Behavior:** Theory X and Theory Y [M. Vanterpool]	To offer participants the opportunity to compare their managerial rhetoric with their behavior. To offer participants the opportunity to explore Theory X and Theory Y assumptions. To offer participants the opportunity to explore behaviors that demonstrate Theory X and Theory Y assumptions. To enable participants to set goals for self-monitored behavior changes and for using rhetoric and behavior that are consistent with Theory Y assumptions.	Two and one-half hours	'91-51

Leadership-Membership/Styles (Continued)

Number	Title [Author]	Goals	Time Required	Volume & Page No.
488	**The Good Leader:** Identifying Effective Behaviors [G. Carline]	To provide the participants with an opportunity to explore different views of leadership. To offer the participants an opportunity to discuss and identify the characteristics and behaviors that contribute to a leader's effectiveness. To encourage the participants to consider how leadership evolves in a group and the effects of various leadership behaviors on group members and task accomplishment.	Approximately two hours and fifteen minutes	'92-37

Leadership-Membership/Motivation

Number	Title [Author]	Goals	Time Required	Volume & Page No.
60	**Dividing the Loot:** Symbolic Feedback	To provide symbolic feedback to participants. To explore the responsibilities and problems of leadership.	One hour	III-49
100	**Motivation:** A Feedback Exercise [D.F. Michalak]	To learn the concepts in Maslow's Need Hierarchy. To get feedback on one's use of motivational techniques in terms of Maslow's Need Hierarchy.	At least one-half hour	'73-43
159	**Fork-Labyrinth:** Leadership Practice [J.F. Veiga]	To diagnose the behavior of leaders and followers in a small group performing a complex competitive task. To teach "on-line" feedback and coaching on leadership behavior. To practice different leadership behaviors.	Approximately three hours	V-53

Leadership-Membership/Motivation (Continued)

Number	Title [Author]	Goals	Time Required	Volume & Page No.
204	**Motivation:** A Supervisory-Skill Activity [K. Frey & J.D. Jackson]	To demonstrate the value of goal setting for task achievement. To demonstrate the positive role of a supervisor in developing the motivation to achieve.	Approximately one hour	VI-28
253	**Penny Pitch:** Demonstrating Reinforcement Style [B.F. Spencer]	To demonstrate how positive or negative reinforcement can affect motivation and task accomplishment. To increase awareness of responses to interventions made by persons with position and status.	Approximately one hour	VII-46
354	**The Manager's Guidebook:** Understanding Motivation [K.L. Murrell]	To provide the participants with a situation in which the issues of motivation can be explored. To help the participants to enhance their understanding of the concept of motivation.	Approximately two and one-half hours	IX-102

Leadership-Membership/Effect on Groups

Number	Title [Author]	Goals	Time Required	Volume & Page No.
35	**Auction:** An Intergroup Competition [J.W. Pfeiffer]	To explore relationships between leadership and decision making in a competitive situation. To illustrate effects of task success or failure on the selection of group representatives and leaders.	Approximately one hour	II-58
41	**Status-Interaction Study:** A Multiple-Role-Play [J.W. Pfeiffer]	To explore effects of status differences and deference on interaction among members.	Forty-five minutes	II-85

Leadership-Membership/Effect on Groups (Continued)

Number	Title [Author]	Goals	Time Required	Volume & Page No.
192	**Package Tour:** Leadership and Consensus Seeking [P. Mumford]	To demonstrate the need for consensus on group goals. To demonstrate leadership techniques and strategies in conducting meetings. To experience the impact of hidden agendas on group decision making.	Approximately two hours	'77-35
195	**Executive Pie:** A Power Experience [S.H. Putnam]	To enhance the awareness of the uses of power in group decision making. To explore the values inherent in various styles of leadership. To simulate a common organizational problem.	Approximately one hour	'77-54
239	**Race from Outer Space:** An Awareness Activity [D.G. Cash]	To compare qualities and skills needed to lead a single racial group and those needed to lead a mixed racial group. To increase awareness of social values and how these may differ among people and groups.	One and one-half to two hours	'79-38
288	**Project Colossus:** Intragroup Competition [J.V. Fee]	To explore the dynamics of status, power, and special knowledge in decision making. To examine the effects of intragroup competition on team functioning.	One to one and one-half hours	'81-43
290	**Dynasell:** Hidden Agendas and Trust [W.W. Kibler]	To demonstrate the impact of distrust on collaboration in a task group. To heighten awareness of one's personal responses when the motives of others are in question.	One and one-half to two hours	'81-50

Leadership-Membership/Effect on Groups (Continued)

Number	Title [Author]	Goals	Time Required	Volume & Page No.
350	**Departmental Dilemma:** Shared Decision Making [J.H. Stevenson]	To increase the participants' awareness of the process and skills involved in shared decision making. To allow the participants to experience shared decision making as a means of conflict management.	Approximately three hours	IX-66
352	**The Company Task Force:** Dealing with Disruptive Behavior [S.W. Whitcomb]	To help the participants to become aware of the roles and behaviors that are disruptive in meetings, the degree to which they are disruptive, and the positive as well as negative consequences associated with each. To offer the participants an opportunity to develop strategies for dealing with disruptive roles and behaviors.	Two and one-half hours	IX-84
382	**Chipping In:** Examining Management Strategies [K. Strauch-Brown]	To demonstrate the effects of managerial behaviors on subordinates. To examine various communication strategies among managers and subordinates. To explore managers' use of resources in helping subordinates.	Two hours and twenty minutes	'85-57
419	**Bean Bags:** Leadership and Group Development [D. Suehs & F. Rogers]	To allow the participants to experience the effects of leadership behavior on a task group. To demonstrate how changes in task, the addition/deletion of staff, and managerial style affect the development and performance of a work group.	One to one and one-half hours	'86-45

Leadership-Membership/Effect on Groups (Continued)

Number	Title [Author]	Goals	Time Required	Volume & Page No.
420	**Position Power:** Exploring the Impact of Role Change [P. Cooke & L.C. Porter]	To explore the effects of power and status on attitudes and performance. To become more aware of how changes in the roles of task-group members affect attitudes and performance.	Approximately three hours	'86-51
421	**Meeting Management:** Coping with Dysfunctional Behaviors [P. Doyle & C.R. Tindal]	To enable the participants to identify dysfunctional behaviors in meetings. To allow the participants to plan and test coping strategies for dealing with such behaviors in meetings.	Approximately one hour for up to four groups. One and one-half hours for five or six groups.	'86-55
442	**Four Corners:** Preferences That Affect Group Work [B. Jameson]	To acquaint the partici-pants with the four essential elements of group work. To explain how these elements interact and how people's preferences for particular elements for particular elements affect group functioning. To provide an opportunity for the participants to increase their awareness of which of the four elements they prefer, which their organi-zations prefer, and the implications of these preferences.	Approximately one hour	'88-51

Communication

Number	Title [Author]	Goals	Time Required	Volume & Page No.
110	**Organization Structures:** Communication Patterns [T. Irwin]	To demonstrate the varying effectiveness of different organization structures. To diagnose working relationships within an intact group. To illustrate less efficient modes of communication. To illustrate perceived alienation.	Approximately one hour	IV-34
139	**Faculty Meeting:** A Multiple Role-Play [F.H. McCarty & B.Nisenholz]	To study behaviors that facilitate and that block communication in groups. To explore the effects of process feedback on team functioning.	Approximately two and one-half hours	'75-15

Values Clarification/Stereotyping

Number	Title [Author]	Goals	Time Required	Volume & Page No.
62	**Polarization:** A Demonstration [J.E. Jones & J.J. Jones]	To explore the experience of interpersonal polarization-its forms and effects. To study conflict management and resolution.	Approximately two hours	III-57
63	**Discrimination:** Simulation Activities	To simulate the experience of discrimination. To study phenomena of stereotyping people.	Varies with each activity	III-62
94	**Traditional American Values:** Intergroup Confrontation	To clarify one's own value system. To explore values held in common within a group. To study differences existing between groups. To begin to remove stereotypes held by members of different groups.	Approximately one and one-half hours	'73-23

Values Clarification/Stereotyping (Continued)

Number	Title [Author]	Goals	Time Required	Volume & Page No.
95	**Sex-Role Stereotyping:** [M. Carson]	To make distinctions between thoughts and feelings about sex-role stereotyping. To examine one's own reactions to sexism in a mixed group. To link feeling feedback to observable behavior. To avoid over-generalization. To explore the experience of interpersonal polarization — its forms and effects. To study conflict resolution.	Approximately two hours	'73-26
113	**Growth Group Values:** A Clarification Exercise [O. Elliott & D. Zellinger]	To clarify one's own value system. To explore values held in common within a group. To study differences existing between groups. To begin to remove stereotypes held by members of different groups.	Approximately one and one-half hours	IV-45
127	**Leadership Characteristics:** Examining Values in Personnel Selection [C.L. Kormanski]	To compare the results of individual decision making. To explore values underlying leadership characteristics. To examine effects of value judgments on personnel selection.	Approximately two hours	'74-13
135	**Kidney Machine:** Group Decision Making [G.M. Phillips]	To explore choices involving values. To study problem-solving procedures in groups. To examine the impact of individuals' values and attitudes on group decision making.	Approximately one hour	'74-78
184	**Sex-Role Attributes:** A Collection of Activities	To expand personal awareness. To explore the cultural biases and prejudices that the sexes have regarding each other.	Varies with each activity	'76-63

Values Clarification/Stereotyping (Continued)

Number	Title [Author]	Goals	Time Required	Volume & Page No.
203	**Headbands:** Group Role Expectations [E. Sieburg]	To experience the pressures of role expecta-tions. To demonstrate the effects of role expectations on individual behavior in a group. To explore the effects of role pressures on total group performance.	Approximately forty-five minutes	VI-25
215	**Who Gets Hired?:** A Male/Female Role Play [L.V. Entrekin & G.N. Soutar]	To clarify one's personal values regarding sex discrimination. To exam-ine the values held in common on this subject within a group. To explore whether groups of different sexual composition have differences in such values. To study the way in which such issues are resolved within a group. To gain insight into the subtle aspects of discrimination.	One to one and one-half hours	VI-106
235	**Who Killed John Doe?:** A Value-Clarification Activity [C.A. Hart]	To articulate individual opinions about social and individual responsibilities. To explore and clarify personal values. To participate in shared decision making.	Approximately one hour	'79-15
248	**Alpha II:** Clarifying Sexual Values [D. Keyworth]	To explore attitudes regarding sexual mores. To compare sexual values with others. To practice group consensus seeking.	Two to two and one-half hours	VII-19

Values Clarification/Stereotyping (Continued)

Number	Title [Author]	Goals	Time Required	Volume & Page No.
258	**Sex-Role Attitudes:** Personal Feedback [B.P. Holleran]	To develop an understanding of the way in which sex-based attitudes influence and are inferred from communication. To discuss attitudes and prejudices about sexes in a nonthreatening environment. To increase awareness of and provide feedback on one's own attitudes, beliefs, and behaviors in regard to sex differences.	Approximately two to three hours	VII-85
338	**Four Cultures:** Exploring Behavioral Expectations [D.L. Gradin]	To explore the effects of cultural behaviors or traits on others. To experience cross-cultural encounters. To increase awareness of how cultural mannerisms and rituals are derived from cultural attitudes.	Two and one-half hours	'83-72
364	**AIRSOPAC:** Choosing a CEO [T.H. Patten, Jr.]	To explore values in executive decision making. To allow the participants to study procedures used by groups to evaluate individual differences among highly qualified people. To examine the impact of individual values and attitudes on group decision making.	Two to two and one-half hours	IX-172

GROUP TASK BEHAVIOR

Problem Solving/Awareness

Number	Title [Author]	Goals	Time Required	Volume & Page No.
7	**Broken Squares:** Nonverbal Problem-Solving	To analyze some aspects of cooperation in solving a group problem. To sensitize participants to behaviors which may contribute toward or obstruct the solving of a group problem.	Approximately forty-five minutes	I-25
102	**Shoe Store:** Group Problem-Solving [A.M. Zelmer]	To observe communication patterns in group problem solving. To explore interpersonal influence in problem solving.	Thirty to sixty minutes	IV-5
103	**Joe Doodlebug:** Group Problem-Solving *[adapted from M. Rokeach]*	To explore the effect of participants' response sets in a group problem-solving activity. To observe leadership behavior in a problem-solving situation.	Approximately forty-five minutes	IV-8
111	**System Problems:** A Diagnostic Activity [M.S. Perlmutter & C.R. Ahrons]	To generate data about the functioning of an intact group or a growth group. To diagnose the way a system approaches problem solving.	Approximately one hour	IV-38
134	**Hung Jury:** A Decision-Making Simulation [S.C. Iman, B.D. Jones, & A.S. Crown]	To study decision-making processes.	Approximately two hours	'74-64
200	**Word-Letter:** A Problem-Solving Activity [J.P. Berliner]	To demonstrate how problems are resolved when the alternatives are not clearly defined or the situation is ambiguous. To explore group problem-solving processes.	Approximately one and one-half hours	VI-15

Problem Solving/Awareness (Continued)

Number	Title [Author]	Goals	Time Required	Volume & Page No.
221	**Numbers:** A Problem-Solving Activity [B.D. Ruben & R.W. Budd]	To demonstrate how new information and assistance can improve performance. To discover how experience facilitates task accomplishment.	One to one and one-half hours	'78-9
240	**Puzzle Cards:** Approaches to Problem Solving [E.J. Cummins]	To generate an interest in and understanding of different approaches to problem solving. To compare advantages and disadvantages of different problem-solving methods.	One to one and one-half hours	'79-41
260	**Island Commission:** Group Problem Solving [P.G. Gillan]	To experience the issues involved in long-range social planning. To study emergent group dynamics and leadership in the completion of a group task. To explore aspects of communication, problem solving, and decision making in a work group.	Two to two and one-half hours	VII-99
285	**Analytical or Creative?:** A Problem-Solving Comparison [B.A. McDonald]	To provide an opportunity to compare analytical and creative problem-solving approaches. To increase awareness of one's own capabilities in and preferences for these two approaches to problem solving.	Approximately one and one-half hours	'81-24

Problem Solving/Awareness (Continued)

Number	Title [Author]	Goals	Time Required	Volume & Page No.
287	**Four-Letter Words:** Examining Task-Group Processes [W.J. Cox]	To study the behavior of an unstructured group in accomplishing a complex task. To heighten awareness of the importance of correct interpretation of written task instructions. To enable group members to compare observed behavior with typical task-group behavior. To assist group members to better perceive and understand individual interactions within a task group.	Approximately two and one-half hours	'81-34
312	**Vacation Schedule:** Group Problem Solving [L.B. Day & M. Blizzard]	To explore the advantages of using group-decision-making procedures to resolve complex issues. To increase awareness of supervisory responsibilities in decision-making situations.	Approximately two hours	VIII-100
313	**Tangram:** Leadership Dimensions [E. Casais]	To identify key functions of a task-team leader. To examine the process of leading a team toward the accomplishment of a task. To experience the information-sharing process within a task team. To provide an opportunity to observe the effects of communication processes on members of a task team.	Approximately two hours	VIII-108

Problem Solving/Awareness (Continued)

Number	Title [Author]	Goals	Time Required	Volume & Page No.
335	**Pebbles:** Vertical and Lateral Problem Solving [D. Muller]	To provide an opportunity to compare vertical and lateral problem-solving approaches. To increase participants' awareness of their preferences for and capabilities in these two approaches to problem solving.	Approximately one and one-half hours	'83-45
337	**The Lawn:** Problem or Symptom? [W.W. Kibler & W.T. Milburn]	To provide an experience in clearly defining a problem. To increase awareness of the difference between the causes of a problem and the symptoms of a problem. To demonstrate how using only oral communication can affect the problem-solving process.	Approximately one and one-half hours	'83-65
430	**There's Never Time To Do It Right:** A Relay Task [R.J. Denz]	To help participants understand the dilemma of quality versus quantity in terms of productivity. To help participants explore the consequences of focusing primarily on quality or quantity in teamwork.	Approximately one hour	'87-45

Problem Solving/Awareness (Continued)

Number	Title [Author]	Goals	Time Required	Volume & Page No.
431	**Unscrambling the Bank Accounts:** Group Problem Solving [J.E. Hebden]	To enable participants to experience group problem-solving processes. To give participants an opportunity to observe and identify behaviors and methods that facilitate or hinder effective teamwork. To highlight the consequences of conflicts between individual objectives and team objectives. To provide a basis for exploring means to make teamwork more effective.	Approximately one hour	'87-51
443	**Orientations:** Left-Brain/Right-Brain Problem Solving [D.J. Nacht, K. Kraiger, & R. Mandrell]	To acquaint the participants with the basic theory of left-brain and right-brain orientations. To provide a way for each participant to determine his or her particular orientation. To examine the ways in which different orientations affect the completion of group tasks. To develop the participants' understanding of the benefits and drawbacks of their own and others' orientations.	Approximately two hours	'88-57

Problem Solving/Awareness (Continued)

Number	Title [Author]	Goals	Time Required	Volume & Page No.
453	**Control or Surrender:** Altering Approaches to Problem Solving [J. Ballard]	To introduce the participants to a method for changing the way in which they perceive problems. To assist the participants in developing action plans in which they apply their changed perceptions to a group-owned problem. To assist the participants in synthesizing their individual action plans into a group approach to dealing with the problem.	Approximately one hour and forty-five minutes	'89-47
454	**Marzilli's Fine Italian Foods:** An Introduction to Strategic Thinking [H.H. Johnson]	To help the participants to become more aware of the assumptions they make in solving problems. To demonstrate the value of suspending assumptions while engaged in problem-solving efforts. To introduce the participants to the concept of strategic thinking and to give them an opportunity to practice it.	Approximately one hour and thirty to forty-five minutes	'89-55
479	**Prairie General Hospital:** Parallel Learning Structures [A.B. Shani & D. Wise]	To help participants to recognize bureaucratic barriers to problem solving within an organization. To demonstrate the use of parallel learning structure interventions toward more optimal utilization of human resources. To help participants to develop methods for cross-boundary organizational dialog mechanisms within bureaucratic structures.	Two and one-half hours	'91-65

Generating Alternatives

Number	Title [Author]	Goals	Time Required	Volume & Page No.
53	**Brainstorming:** A Problem-Solving Activity	To generate an extensive number of ideas or solutions to a problem by suspending criticism and evaluation. To develop skills in creative problem solving.	Approximately one hour	III-14
76	**Quaker Meeting**	To generate a large number of ideas, suggestions, approaches to a problem or topic when the group is too large to employ brainstorming techniques. To gather data quickly for a large group to process.	Fifteen minutes for the actual "Quaker meeting" plus processing time appropriate for the particular group	'72-11
141	**Nominal Group Technique:** An Applied Group Problem-Solving Activity [D.L. Ford, Jr.; *adapted from A. Delbecq & A. Van de Ven]*	To increase creativity and participation in group meetings involving problem-solving and/or fact-finding tasks. To develop or expand perception of critical issues within problem areas. To identify priorities of selected issues within problems, considering the viewpoints of differently oriented groups.	Two hours	'75-35
185	**Poems:** Interpersonal Communication [B.P Holleran]	To experience the interaction conditions necessary for creative problem solving. To arrive at a creative solution in a group situation.	One to one and one-half hours	'77-13

Generating Alternatives (Continued)

Number	Title [Author]	Goals	Time Required	Volume & Page No.
343	**Bricks:** Creative Problem Solving [J.A. Tyler]	To provide the participants with an opportunity to practice creative problem solving. To allow the participants to experience the dynamics that are involved in group-task accomplishment.	Approximately one and one-half hours	IX-10
370	**QC Agenda:** Collaborative Problem Identification [M.J. Miller]	To introduce the process by which quality circles identify and select work-related problems as projects. To allow the participants to practice behaviors that are associated with effective circle membership: participating collaboratively in circle efforts, listening to other members, and withholding judgment while considering issues that are before the circle.	Approximately one and one-half hours	'84-44
467	**Cooperative Inventions:** Fostering Creativity [R.W. Russell]	To allow the participants to examine their individual approaches to creating ideas. To offer the participants an opportunity to share and learn methods of completing a creative task that requires a joint effort. To help the participants to gain insight into factors that inhibit creativity as well as ones that foster creativity.	Approximately forty minutes	'90-61

Group Feedback

Number	Title [Author]	Goals	Time Required	Volume & Page No.
17	**Leveling:** Giving and Receiving Adverse Feedback [J.W. Pfeiffer]	To let participants compare their perceptions of how a group sees them with the actual feedback obtained from the group. To legitimize giving negative feedback within a group. To develop skills in giving negative feedback.	Approximately ten minutes per participant	I-79
18	**Dependency-Intimacy:** A Feedback Experience [J.E. Jones]	To provide instrumented feedback. To study how the personal dimensions of dependency and intimacy affect group development.	Approximately one and one-half hours	I-82
38	**Role Nominations:** A Feedback Experience *[based on K.D. Benne & P. Sheats]*	To provide feedback to group members on the roles fellow members see them playing. To study various types of roles in relation to group goals. To demonstrate that leadership in a small group consists of several functions which should be shared among members.	Approximately one and one-half hours	II-72
57	**Nominations:** Personal Instrumented Feedback	To provide feedback to group members on how they are perceived by each other. To analyze the climate and the norms of the group by studying members' behavior, composition of the group, and members' expectations of each other.	Approximately one hour	III-33

Group Feedback (Continued)

Number	Title [Author]	Goals	Time Required	Volume & Page No.
66	**Team-Building:** A Feedback Experience	To help an intact work group diagnose its functioning. To establish a cooperative expectation within a task group. To assist a "real life" group or business manager (leader, chairman, supervisor) to develop norms of openness, trust, and interdependence among team members and/or members of his organization.	A minimum of one day	III-73
84	**Psychomat**	To provide an atmosphere in which participants can encounter each other in a variety of ways. To encourage creative, sensitive risk taking on the part of participants. To explore reactions to a highly unstructured interpersonal situation.	Six to nine hours	'72-58
104	**The Gift of Happiness:** Experience Positive Feedback [D. Keyworth]	To promote a climate of trust, self-worth, and positive reinforcement within a small group. To experience giving and receiving positive feedback in a nonthreatening way.	Approximately five minutes per participant and about thirty minutes for processing.	IV-15
118	**Twenty-Five Questions:** A Team Development Exercise [J.E. Jones]	To enhance work relationships in intact groups. To stimulate group discussion about work-related topics. To clarify assumptions that team members make about each other.	Approximately one and one-half hours	IV-88

Group Feedback (Continued)

Number	Title [Author]	Goals	Time Required	Volume & Page No.
291	**I Hear That You...:** Giving and Receiving Feedback [D.P. Danko & R. Cherry]	To establish a climate conducive to giving and receiving feedback in established work groups. To practice active listening and feedback skills. To help make work-group behavior more understandable by linking behavior to perceptions. To improve work-group relations and climate.	One and one-half to two hours	'81-54
316	**Group Sociogram:** Intragroup Communication [T.J. Mallinson]	To identify existing patterns of interaction and influence in an intact group. To increase awareness of the effects of group dynamics on intragroup communication patterns.	Approximately one and one-half hours	VIII-131
326	**The Car:** Feedback on Group Membership Styles [A.A. Wells]	To allow the members of an ongoing work group to obtain feedback on their perceived role functions and membership styles. To enable a group to examine its operating style and to plan changes. To encourage and practice giving and receiving feedback.	Approximately one and one-half hours	'82-55
345	**Constructive Criticism:** Rating Leadership Abilities [F.E. Woodall]	To provide an opportunity for the members of an intact group to give and receive feedback regarding their leadership abilities. To give the members experience in evaluating themselves and others in a constructive, concrete manner.	One and one-half to two hours	IX-28

Group Feedback (Continued)

Number	Title [Author]	Goals	Time Required	Volume & Page No.
356	**Messages:** A Group Feedback Experience [G.L Talbot]	To examine the thought process, verbal behavior, and risk factor involved in sending verbal messages about feelings. To analyze the ways in which the process of sending and receiving such messages contributes to group cohesiveness.	Approximately forty-five minutes	IX-110
403	**Yearbook:** Positive Group Feedback [B. Ketcham & A. Gilburg]	To allow the members of an ongoing group to give and receive positive feedback about their perceived roles within the group. To enhance the members' appreciation of themselves and one another. To help the members to determine ways in which group functioning might be improved in the future.	One hour and forty minutes to two hours	X-92
404	**Healthy or Unhealthy?:** Assessing Group Functioning	To offer the participants an opportunity to assess the health of their group in terms of functional and dysfunctional member behaviors and to provide the group with feedback about this assessment. To assist the participants in developing group definitions of a "healthy" group and an "unhealthy" group. To help the participants to establish action steps to take to improve their group's functioning.	Approximately two hours and fifteen minutes	X-96

Group Feedback (Continued)

Number	Title [Author]	Goals	Time Required	Volume & Page No.
405	**Sticky Wickets:** Exploring Group Stress [W.B. Kline & J.J. Blase]	To develop the participants' awareness of the factors that can lead to group stress. To allow the participants to experience some of these factors. To offer the participants an opportunity to share with one another their ideas for dealing with group stress.	One hour and forty-five minutes to two hours	X-99
444	**The Advertising Firm:** A Group Feedback Activity [J. Lindholm]	To develop the participants' awareness of how they work together while completing a task. To assist the participants in generating ways to improve their effectiveness as a group. To monitor the effect of periodic feedback on an intact group as it completes a task. To enhance the participants' understanding of the role of feedback in enhancing a group's effectiveness.	Approximately one and one-half hours	'88-69
445	**Images:** Envisioning the Ideal Group [J.E. Garcia & K.S. Keleman]	To provide an opportunity for the members of an intact group to receive feedback from one another about the perceived image of the group. To enable the members to examine the behaviors that lead to particular images of a group. To assist the members in developing images by which they would like their group to be known. To help the members to develop ways of actualizing these images.	Two to two and one-half hours	'00-73

Group Feedback (Continued)

Number	Title [Author]	Goals	Time Required	Volume & Page No.
455	**America's Favorite Pastime:** Clarifying Role Perceptions [T. Hildebrandt]	To identify the various roles that exist in a team. To provide a means for sharing the team members' perceptions of their roles. To develop the members' awareness of their own contributions to the team as well as the contributions of fellow team members. To assist the team members in identifying ways to use their perceptions of their own and one another's roles to improve team functioning.	One hour and forty-five minutes to two hours	'89-61
456	**It's in the Cards:** Sharing Team Perceptions [F.A. Miller, J.H. Katz, & A.A. Schnidman]	To help the participants to clarify how they perceive (1) themselves as team members, (2) their fellow team members, (3) the team as whole, and (4) the team's relationship to the organization.	Approximately three hours, depending on the size of the group	'89-67

Group Feedback (Continued)

Number	Title [Author]	Goals	Time Required	Volume & Page No.
468	**The Genie's Wish:** Identifying and Addressing Group Needs [T.F. Penderghast]	To offer the participants an opportunity to identify what they need, both individually and as a group, in order to work effectively and productively and to learn ways in which those needs might be met. To surface important group issues and to encourage group growth. to foster the participants' problem-solving skills. To offer the participants an opportunity to practice visualizing (as a part of the guided-imagery process). To help the participants understand their individual task approaches and how the combination of these different approaches can enhance the group problem-solving process.	A minimum of two hours and fifteen minutes, based on a five-member group (A period of ten minutes extra is required for each additional member over five)	'90-67
469	**Symbols:** Sharing Role Perceptions [P. Doyle]	To familiarize the participants with the various roles that exist in a work team. To provide the participants with the opportunity to share perceptions of their roles in their work team. To provide the participants with the opportunity to practice giving and receiving feedback.	Approximately one hour and fifteen minutes	'90-73

Group Feedback (Continued)

Number	Title [Author]	Goals	Time Required	Volume & Page No.
480	**Multiple Roles:** Nature and Orientation [M. Nandy]	To develop the participants' awareness of multiple roles in groups. To offer participants a system for categorizing the nature and orientation of group roles. To offer participants the opportunity to determine ways to improve group functioning in the future.	Approximately two hours	'91-85
489	**Group Calendar:** Celebrating Significant Events [M.B. Sokol & D.A. Cohen]	To offer the participants a nonthreatening method of getting to know one another better. To give the participants the opportunity to remember significant work-related events that took place during the past year and to recognize and appreciate one another's achievements. To allow the participants to compare memories of significant work-related events.	One hour to one hour and fifteen minutes	'92-47

Group Feedback (Continued)

Number	Title [Author]	Goals	Time Required	Volume & Page No.
490	**Strengths and Needs:** Using Feedback for Group Development [T. Burchett]	To provide an opportunity for the participants to give one another feedback about the strengths they bring to their work group. To offer the participants a chance to identify what they like on the job and what they would like to change and then to share this information with one another. To provide a structure through which the participants can express what they need from one another. To provide an opportunity for the participants to do action planning based on their strengths, likes, items they would like to change, and needs.	This activity is conducted in two sessions. Session 1, sharing feedback, requires two to three and one-half hours, depending on the size of the work group. Session 2, action planning based on the information shared in the first session, requires approximately three hours	'92-51

Competition (Win-Lose)

Number	Title [Author]	Goals	Time Required	Volume & Page No.
32	**Model-Building:** An Intergroup Competition	To study interpersonal and intergroup competition phenomena. To explore the feeling content and behavioral results of winning and losing. To provide feedback to group members on their contributions in a task situation.	Approximately one and one-half hours	II-29

Competition (Win-Lose) (Continued)

Number	Title [Author]	Goals	Time Required	Volume & Page No.
54	**Towers:** An Intergroup Competition	To study phenomena of competition among groups. To explore the feeling content and behavioral outcomes of winning and losing. To provide a basis for feedback to group members on their relations with other group members and their productivity in a task situation.	Approximately one and one-half hours	III-17
81	**Intergroup Model-Building:** The Lego Man [W.B. Reddy & O. Kroeger]	To extract the learnings from a competitive teamwork experience, in terms of leadership style, developing alternatives, dominance and submission within teams, and distribution of work and resources. To diagnose the dynamics of an intact group in terms of role taking.	Approximately two hours	'72-36
105	**Wooden Blocks:** A Competition Exercise [A.M. Zelmer]	To explore individual and small group goal-setting behavior and achievement motivation. To study interpersonal and intergroup competition phenomena. To explore feelings and outcomes of winning and losing.	Approximately one hour	IV-18
150	**Riddles:** Intergroup Competition [B.P. Holleran]	To observe competitive behavior among groups. To determine how a group interacts with other groups when it is dependent on them for the completion of its task.	Approximately one and one-half hours	V-5

Competition (Win-Lose) (Continued)

Number	Title [Author]	Goals	Time Required	Volume & Page No.
161	**Lego Bridge:** Intergroup Competition [P. Mumford]	To observe spontaneous patterns of organization in work groups. To explore the relationship between planning and production. To study the effects of inter-group competition on team functioning.	Approximately one and one-half hours	V-73
210	**Darts:** Competition and Motivation [S. Dolinsky]	To develop awareness of the factors involved in motivation. To increase awareness of the effects of motivation/incentives on the attitudes and perfor-mance of a given task in an intergroup competitive situation.	Approximately one and one-half hours	VI-61
218	**Spy:** An Intergroup Activity [S.J. Schoen]	To explore the impact of competition between groups. To demonstrate different methods of group problem solving. To exam-ine the dynamics of suspi-cion and distrust in a group. To observe the process of a leaderless group in the completion of a specific task.	Approximately one and one-half hours	VI-117
256	**Slingshots:** Studying Group Dynamics [K.M. Bond]	To experience the group dynamics involved in task accomplishment. To study the effects of competition on group functioning. To experience the functional and dysfunctional aspects of process interventions.	Approximately one hour and fifteen minutes	VII-69

Competition (Win-Lose) (Continued)

Number	Title [Author]	Goals	Time Required	Volume & Page No.
308	**Structures:** Intergroup Competition [A.C. Stein, S.C. Iman, & A.A. Ramos]	To study the effects of intergroup competition on group processes. To identify helps and hindrances to task accomplishment. To demonstrate the impact of effective and ineffective communication processes in task groups.	Approximately two hours	VIII-69
311	**Risk Game:** Competition and Team Building	To increase awareness of one's preferred level of risk taking. To increase awareness of how the attitudes of others can affect one's choices and level of risk taking. To study the effects of intergroup competition on intragroup communication processes.	Approximately two hours	VIII-93

Competition and Collaboration (Win-Lose/Win-Win)

Number	Title [Author]	Goals	Time Required	Volume & Page No.
36	**Win As Much As You Can:** An Intergroup Competition *[based on W. Gellerman]*	To dramatize the merits of both competitive and collaborative models within the context of intragroup and intergroup relations. To illustrate the impact of win-lose situations.	Approximately one hour	II-62
61	**Prisoner's Dilemma:** An Intergroup Competition	To explore trust between group members and effects of betrayal of trust. To demonstrate effects of interpersonal competition. To dramatize the merit of a collaborative posture in intragroup and intergroup relations.	Approximately one hour	III-52

Competition and Collaboration (Win-Lose/Win-Win) (Continued)

Number	Title [Author]	Goals	Time Required	Volume & Page No.
78	**Unequal Resources**	To provide an opportunity for observing group use of resources which have been distributed unequally. To observe bargaining processes.	Approximately one hour	'72-17
83	**Decisions:** An Intergroup Negotiation [H.I. Feir, with R.J. Turner, R. Cox, D.N. Kanouse, & R.G. Mason]	To experience the issues surrounding intergroup trust building and trust betrayal. To explore considerations of inter-group competition versus collaboration. To examine limited communication under stress. To study negotiation and negotia-tion strategies. To consider group decision-making processes.	A minimum of four and one-half hours	'72-51
147	**World Bank:** An Intergroup Negotiation [N.H. Berkowitz & H.A. Hornstein]	To experience the conflict between advantages of cooperation and advan-tages of competition in a mixed-motive dilemma. To explore some dynamics of trust between groups. To practice negotiation skills.	Approximately three hours	'75-56
164	**Testing:** Intergroup Competition [P.R. Scholtes]	To explore the impact of the lack of communication in competitive situations. To demonstrate the need for collaboration and interdependence.	Approximately one and one-half hours	V-91
165	**Marbles:** A Community Experiment *[adapted from F.L. Goodman]*	To study community from the perspectives of estab-lishing, enforcing, and interpreting rules. To explore rule-governed behaviors.	Approximately two hours	V-98

Competition and Collaboration (Win-Lose/Win-Win) (Continued)

Number	Title [Author]	Goals	Time Required	Volume & Page No.
178	**Al Kohbari:** An Information-Sharing Multiple Role Play [R.E. Mattingly]	To study how information relevant to a task is shared within work groups. To observe problem-solving strategies within work groups. To explore the effects of collaboration and competition in group problem solving. To demonstrate the effects of hidden agendas on group decision making.	Approximately two hours	'76-26
179	**X-Y:** A Three-Way Intergroup Competition [G.J. Rath, J. Kisch, & H.E. Miller]	To explore interpersonal trust. To demonstrate the effects of cooperation, competition, and betrayal. To dramatize the advantages of both competitive and collaborative models in intergroup relations.	Approximately two hours	'76-41
189	**Blue/Green:** An Intergroup Negotiation *[adapted from J. Owens]*	To explore the element of trust between group members and the effects of the betrayal of trust. To demonstrate the effects of competition and collaboration in intergroup relationships. To study the effects of win-lose, win-win, and lose-lose strategies in negotiations between groups.	One and one-half hours	'77-24
205	**Circle in the Square:** A Cooperation/ Competition Activity [C.E. Lee]	To demonstrate how cooperation and competition can affect winning and losing. To explore how winning and losing are defined, perceived, and measured.	Approximately one hour	VI-32

Competition and Collaboration (Win-Lose/Win-Win) (Continued)

Number	Title [Author]	Goals	Time Required	Volume & Page No.
212	**Murder One:** Information Sharing [D.K. McLeod]	To explore the effects of cooperation-collaboration versus competition in group problem solving. To demonstrate the need for information sharing and other problem-solving strategies in a task-oriented group. To study the roles that emerge in a task group.	One and one-half hours	VI-75
231	**Balance of Power:** A Cooperation/ Competition Activity [L. Parshall]	To explore the effects of collaboration and competition strategies in group problem solving. To study how task-relevant information is shared between groups. To increase awareness of the influence that leaders (or political systems) have on decision making in groups.	Approximately two and one-half hours	'78-63
237	**Line of Four:** An Intergroup Competition [W.R. Mulford]	To examine a group's communication, planning, and collaborative behavior. To examine the use of self-imposed rules of behavior. To explore the dynamics of intergroup competition.	Approximately one and one-half hours	'79-21
243	**Paper Box:** An Intergroup Competition Activity [J.G. Clawson]	To study intra- and inter-group relations and conflict. To demonstrate the effects of collaboration versus those of competition. To demonstrate the impact of negotiation on collaborative activities. To practice intragroup planning and problem-solving processes.	Two and one-half to three hours	'79-60

Competition and Collaboration (Win-Lose/Win-Win) (Continued)

Number	Title [Author]	Goals	Time Required	Volume & Page No.
263	**Trading Cards:** A Power Simulation [J. Proescher]	To experience the consequences of conflict between group goals and goals of individual members. To experience inter-group and intragroup competition. To identify patterns of competition and cooperation among group members in a stressful situation. To identify how group and individual strategies affect the group's attainment of a goal.	One and one-half to two hours	VII-112
264	**War Gaming:** An Intergroup Competition [A.J. Schuh]	To study group decision making and interaction under stress. To examine the importance of coopera-tion in small-group work. To demonstrate the effects of win-win and win-lose approaches to intergroup conflict.	Two to four hours	VII-117
265	**Monetary Investment:** Negotiation [T. Armor]	To provide insight into the dynamics of negotiation processes: strategy, constituent pressure, consensus, and mediation. To simulate a collective bargaining experience. To explore the behavior of participants in a bargaining situation.	One and one-half to two hours	VII-124

Competition and Collaboration (Win-Lose/Win-Win) (Continued)

Number	Title [Author]	Goals	Time Required	Volume & Page No.
278	**Move to Newtown:** A Collaboration Activity [R. Parker & A.H. Hartenstein]	To increase awareness of the dynamics of competition and collaboration. To experience the effects of the use of role power in negotiation situations. To explore the effects of role expectations on behavior and reactions. To practice renegotiation of role responsibilities and expectations within a work unit.	A minimum of three hours	'80-60
279	**Creative Products:** Intergroup Conflict Resolution [W.J. Heisler & R.W. Shively]	To examine the effects of collaboration and competition in intergroup relationships. To demonstrate the effects of win-win and win-lose approaches to intergroup conflict. To practice intragroup planning and problem solving.	Two and one-half to three hours	'80-69
280	**High Iron:** Collaboration and Competition [D.T. Simpson]	To examine the elements of negotiation and collaboration in achieving goals. To experience the effects of collaboration and/or competition in problem solving.	Approximately two hours	'80-78
314	**Territory:** Intergroup Negotiation [P. Cooke & A.J. Reilly]	To experience the effects of a negotiation activity. To increase awareness of various negotiation strategies. To practice collaboration strategies in intergroup problem solving.	Approximately two and one-half hours	VIII-120

Competition and Collaboration (Win-Lose/Win-Win) (Continued)

Number	Title [Author]	Goals	Time Required	Volume & Page No.
383	**The Welsh Boothouse:** Intergroup Competition and Collaboration [K.J. Bowdery]	To study the sharing of information in a task-oriented group. To examine the types of member and leader behaviors that emerge as a group works on solving a problem. To demonstrate the effects of competition and collaboration in intergroup relationships. To demonstrate the effects of using group representatives as negotiators in intergroup relationships.	Approximately two and one-half hours	'85-67
432	**Society of Taos:** Group Decision Making [M.W. Cooney]	To allow the participants to experience problem-solving and decision-making strategies within a group. To offer the participants an opportunity to study how task-relevant information is shared within a group. To demonstrate the effects that individual priorities can have on group decision.	Approximately two hours	'87-57
457	**The Candy Bar:** Using Power Strategies [J.H. Farr & S.H. Howarth]	To acquaint the participants with seven bases of power (French & Raven, 1959; Hersey, Blanchard, & Natemeyer, 1979; Raven & Kruglanski, 1975): coercive power, connection power, expert power, information power, legitimate power, referent power, and reward power. To offer the participants an opportunity to experience and compare the effects of strategies associated with the seven bases of power.	Approximately one and one-half hours	'89-73

Competition and Collaboration (Win-Lose/Win-Win) (Continued)

Number	Title [Author]	Goals	Time Required	Volume & Page No.
470	**Greenback Financial Services:** Competitive or Collaborative Problem Solving? [J.E. Hebden]	To offer the participants an opportunity to experience a group problem-solving situation. To assist the participants in identifying the feelings evoked by different problem-solving techniques. To help the participants to determine when competition and collaboration are appropriate as problem-solving strategies. To encourage the participants to analyze the effectiveness of their own problem-solving techniques.	One and one-half to two hours	'90-83
491	**Whirlybird:** Examining Competition and Collaboration [G. Gemmill & G. Wagenheim]	To offer the participants an opportunity to experience and explore both intragroup collaboration and intergroup competition. To encourage the participants' creativity. To facilitate team building within individual subgroups through the completion of a collaborative task.	One hour and fifteen to thirty minutes	'92-63

Collaboration (Win-Win)

Number	Title [Author]	Goals	Time Required	Volume & Page No.
31	**Lutts and Mipps:** Group Problem-Solving *[based on Rimoldi]*	To study the sharing of information in a task-oriented group. To focus on cooperation in group problem solving. To observe the emergence of leadership behavior in group problem solving.	Approximately forty-five minutes	II-24

Collaboration (Win-Win) (Continued)

Number	Title [Author]	Goals	Time Required	Volume & Page No.
80	**Energy International:** A Problem-Solving Multiple Role-Play	To study how task-relevant information is shared within a work group. To observe problem-solving strategies within a group. To explore the effects of collaboration and competition in group problem solving.	Approximately two hours	'72-25
117	**Pine County:** Information-Sharing [L. Dunn]	To explore the effects of collaboration and competition in group problem solving. To study how task-relevant information is shared within a work group. To observe problem-solving strategies within a group. To demonstrate the impact of various leadership styles on task accomplishment.	Approximately one hour	IV-75
133	**Farm E-Z:** A Multiple-Role-Play, Problem-Solving Experience [J.L. Joyce]	To study the sharing of information in task-oriented groups. To learn to distinguish a true problem from those which are only symptomatic. To observe problem-solving strategies within a group.	Approximately two hours	'74-44
155	**Sales Puzzle:** Information Sharing *[adapted from A.A. Zoll III]*	To explore the effects of collaboration and competition in group problem solving. To study how information is shared by members of a work group. To observe problem-solving strategies within a group.	Approximately one hour	V-34

Collaboration (Win-Win) (Continued)

Number	Title [Author]	Goals	Time Required	Volume & Page No.
156	**Room 703:** Information Sharing [J.R. Joachim]	To explore the effects of collaboration and competition in group problem solving. To study how task-relevant information is shared within a work group. To observe group strategies for problem solving.	Thirty to forty-five minutes	V-39
284	**Farmers:** Information Sharing [A. Kuperman]	To demonstrate the effects of collaboration and information sharing in problem solving. To explore aspects of collaboration such as verbal communication and division of labor.	Approximately two hours	'81-16
302	**Cross-Group Negotiation and Cooperation:** Studying Group Dynamics [B.L. Fisher & R.G. Sachs]	To provide an opportunity to experience the effects of cooperation in task group functioning. To explore the effects of conflicting objectives on the behavior of members of a task group. To increase awareness of the positive effects of planning, negotiation, and sharing of resources among work-group members.	Approximately one and one-half hours	VIII-41
319	**Intertwine:** Intergroup Collaboration [M. Sashkin]	To illustrate intergroup task interdependence. To explore aspects of collaboration such as communication and division of labor. To practice intergroup problem-solving skills.	Approximately one and one-half to two hours	'82-20

Collaboration (Win-Win) (Continued)

Number	Title [Author]	Goals	Time Required	Volume & Page No.
320	**Block Buster:** A Collaboration Activity [R.M. Thompson]	To experience elements of teamwork in group problem solving. To examine the effects of planning on task achievement. To examine the significance of communication and rhythm in a particular type of group task.	One and one-half to two hours	'82-24
359	**The Sales Manager's Journey:** Group Problem Solving [G. Fielding]	To study the sharing of information in a task-oriented group. To examine the various types of member behavior that emerge as a group works on solving a problem.	One and one-half hours	IX-125
384	**Stock Exchange:** A Collaboration Activity [K.W. Howard]	To provide the participants with an opportunity to experience the effects of different approaches to developing resources. To develop the participants' awareness of the advantages and disadvantages of various collaborative strategies.	One hour and forty minutes	'85-75
481	**Puzzling Encounters:** Creative Brainstorming [B. Harville]	To help the participants to explore elements of teamwork in group problem solving. To help the participants to explore how to develop creative abilities in a group setting. To provide an opportunity for participants to compare individual creativity with group brainstorming activities.	One hour and forty-five minutes	'91-97

Collaboration (Win-Win) (Continued)

Number	Title [Author]	Goals	Time Required	Volume & Page No.
482	**Dust Pan Case:** Solving the Mystery [A.E. Dickinson]	To help the participants to become aware of the importance of communication and information sharing in groups. To develop the participants' awareness of how they share information while completing a task. To provide the participants with an opportunity to study how information is shared by members of a group.	One and one-half hours	'91-107

Conflict Resolution/Values Polarization

Number	Title [Author]	Goals	Time Required	Volume & Page No.
14	**Conflict Resolution:** A Collection of Tasks	To generate data about how groups resolve conflict.	Varies with each activity	I-70
158	**Absentee:** A Management Role Play [R.J. Carpenter, Jr.]	To explore the dynamics of decision making. To study the resolution and management of conflict. To reveal loyalty patterns among peers and superiors.	Approximately one and one-half hours	V-49
217	**Negotiating Differences:** Avoiding Polarization [D.X. Swenson]	To identify the dimensions along which people may differ. To explore the potential for persons to complement as well as conflict with each other, as a result of such differences. To negotiate a contract for coordinating different personal styles or opinions.	Approximately one hour	VI-114

Conflict Resolution/Values Polarization (Continued)

Number	Title [Author]	Goals	Time Required	Volume & Page No.
224	**Controversial Issues:** Case Studies in Conflict [J.T. Wood]	To examine the effects of conflict on members of problem-solving groups. To acquaint members with alternative methods of coping with conflict in groups. To examine individual styles of handling conflicts and their effects among members of problem-solving groups.	Approximately one and one-half to two hours	'78-28
267	**Whom To Choose:** Values and Group Decision Making [C.L. Eveland & D.M. Hai]	To examine and make choices concerning one's own values. To assess the degree to which members of a group have common values and the impact of this on group decision making. To observe problem-solving strategies in groups.	Forty-five minutes to one hour	VII-141
323	**Budget Cutting:** Conflict and Consensus Seeking [T.L. Maris]	To experience the dynamics of consensus seeking in a decision-making group. To provide experience in establishing priorities. To explore methods for resolving conflict in decision-making groups. To examine individual ways of handling conflict in groups.	Approximately two and one-half hours	'82-35

Conflict Resolution/Values Polarization (Continued)

Number	Title [Author]	Goals	Time Required	Volume & Page No.
406	**Ajax Appliance Corporation:** Exploring Conflict-Management Styles [J.L. Grewell, M.L. Gracey, G. Platt, & D.N. DeHaven]	To illustrate various approaches to managing conflict and the ways in which these approaches affect the process of resolving a problem. To offer the participants opportunities to practice assigned approaches and to experiment with alternative approaches during role plays involving conflict.	Two hours and twenty minutes	X-106
407	**The Value Profile:** Legitimizing Intergroup Differences [E.F. Pajak]	To help two work groups within an organization to understand and accept the legitimacy of each other's values so that they can interact more effectively. To assist each group in establishing its own profile of values.	One hour and forty-five minutes to two hours	X-118
471	**Bargaining, United Nations Style:** Exploring the Impact of Cultural Values [J.I. Oliver & J.E. Oliver]	To offer each participant an opportunity to experience being a person from a different culture. To offer the participants an opportunity to interact with people who represent a different culture. To demonstrate the effects of cultural differences on interactions between members of different cultures. To allow the participants to experience the process of negotiation between two people whose values differ.	Approximately two to two and one-half hours	'90-95

Conflict Resolution/Values Polarization (Continued)

Number	Title [Author]	Goals	Time Required	Volume & Page No.
483	**Conflict Management:** Developing a Procedure [L.C. Porter]	To acquaint the members of an intact work group with some guidelines for resolving a conflict with another person by giving useful feedback. To help the group members to develop their own procedure for managing conflict.	One hour and forty-five minutes to two hours and fifteen minutes	'91-119
492	**Zenoland:** Managing Culture Clash [J. Lobasz-Mavromatis]	To encourage the participants to consider the impact of cultural diversity on interactions among people. To foster the participants' awareness of and sensitivity to cultural attitudes and behaviors that are different from their own. To provide an opportunity for the participants to practice communicating and problem solving in a culturally diverse setting.	Approximately two hours and forty-five minutes	'92-69

Consensus/Synergy

Number	Title [Author]	Goals	Time Required	Volume & Page No.
11	**Top Problems:** A Consensus-Seeking Task [J.J. Sherwood]	To compare the results of individual decision making with the results of group decision making. To teach effective consensus-seeking behaviors in task groups.	Approximately one and one-half hours	I-49
12	**Choosing a Color:** A Multiple-Role-Play [J.W. Pfeiffer]	To explore behavioral responses to an ambiguous task. To demonstrate the effects of shared leadership.	Approximately forty-five minutes	I-56

Consensus/Synergy (Continued)

Number	Title [Author]	Goals	Time Required	Volume & Page No.
15	**Residence Halls:** A Consensus-Seeking Task	To study the degree to which members of a group agree on certain values. To assess the decision-making norms of the group. To identify the "natural leadership" functioning in the group.	Approximately one hour	I-72
30	**NORC:** A Consensus-Seeking Task [J.E. Jones]	To compare results of individual decision making and of group decision making. To generate data to discuss decision-making patterns in task groups.	Approximately one hour	II-18
30	**Kerner Report:** A Consensus-Seeking Task	To compare the results of individual decision making with the results of group decision making. To generate data to discuss decision-making patterns in task groups. To diagnose the level of development in a task group.	Approximately one hour	III-64
69	**Supervisory Behavior/Aims of Education:** Consensus-Seeking Tasks *[worksheets adapted from D. Nylen, J.R. Mitchell, & A. Stout]*	To explore the relationships between subjective involvement with issues and problem solving. To teach effective consensus-seeking behaviors in task groups.	Approximately one and one-half hours	III-84
77	**Team Identity** [J.E. Jones]	To develop cohesion within work groups established as part of a larger training group. To explore the dynamics of group task accomplishment.	Approximately one and one-half hours	'72-13

Consensus/Synergy (Continued)

Number	Title [Author]	Goals	Time Required	Volume & Page No.
115	**Consensus-Seeking:** A Collection of Tasks *[worksheets by D. Keyworth, J.J. Sherwood, J.E. Jones, T. White, M. Carson, B. Rainbow, A. Dew, S. Pavletich, R.D. Jorgenson, & B. Holmberg]*	To teach effective consensus-seeking behaviors in task groups. To explore the concept of synergy in reference to outcomes of group decision making.	Approximately one hour	IV-51
140	**Lost at Sea:** A Consensus-Seeking Task *[P.M. Nemiroff & W.A. Pasmore]*	To teach the effectiveness of consensus-seeking behavior in task groups through comparative experiences with both individual decision making and group decision making. To explore the concepts of synergy in reference to the outcomes of group decision making.	Approximately one hour	'75-28
151	**Cash Register:** Group Decision Making *[based on W.V. Haney]*	To demonstrate how decision making is improved by consensus-seeking. To explore the impact that assumptions have on decision making.	Approximately thirty minutes	V-10
157	**Letter Occurrence/Health Professions Prestige:** Consensus-Seeking Tasks *[K.D. Scott & J.W. Pfeiffer]*	To compare decisions made by individuals with those made by groups. To teach effective consensus-seeking techniques. To demonstrate the phenomenon of synergy.	Approximately one hour per task	V-44
177	**Wilderness Survival:** A Consensus-Seeking Task *[D.T. Simpson]*	To teach effective consensus-seeking behaviors in task groups. To explore the concepts of synergy as it relates to outcomes of group decision making.	Approximately one and one-half hours	'76-19

Consensus/Synergy (Continued)

Number	Title [Author]	Goals	Time Required	Volume & Page No.
187	**Pyramids:** A Consensus Experience [R.J. Carpenter, Jr.]	To study the consensus process within an organizational hierarchy. To allow participants to define organizational concepts individually and through an organizational process of small-group pyramiding. To explore the dynamics of influence and power within groups and organizations.	Approximately two hours	'77-20
223	**Admissions Committee:** A Consensus-Seeking Activity [W.J. Heisler]	To compare decisions made by individuals with those made by groups. To teach effective consensus-seeking techniques. To teach the concepts of synergy.	Approximately one and one-half to two hours	'78-15
236	**Alphabet Names:** Achieving Synergy in Task Groups [R.P. Greco]	To allow participants to experience the effects of synergy on group tasks. To explore the relationship between group commitment to a task and synergy.	Forty-five minutes to one hour	'79-19
255	**Lists:** A Collection of Consensus Activities [B.D. Leskin]	To allow participants to practice giving and receiving feedback. To practice effective consensus-seeking behavior in groups. To demonstrate that relevant performance data from interdependent tasks is widely rather than narrowly shared by group members.	Two and one-half to three hours	VII-57

Consensus/Synergy (Continued)

Number	Title [Author]	Goals	Time Required	Volume & Page No.
271	**Values for the 1980s:** Consensus Seeking [L.D. Goodstein, W.W. Burke, & P. Cooke]	To provide an opportunity to explore differences between individual and group decision-making processes. To practice consensus-seeking behavior in groups. To explore group members' social values.	Approximately three hours	'80-20

ORGANIZATIONS

Awareness/Diagnosis

Number	Title [Author]	Goals	Time Required	Volume & Page No.
40	**Force-Field Analysis:** Individual Problem-Solving *[based on W.G. Bennis & S. Eisen]*	To study dimensions of problems and to devise strategies for solving them through diagram and analysis. To experience the consultative role.	Approximately two and one-half hours	II-79
67	**Organizational Mirror:** A Feedback Experience	To generate data that can permit an organization to diagnose its functioning. To establish avenues of feedback between an organization and other groups with which it is linked.	Approximately two hours	III-78
73	**Wahoo City:** A Role Alternation [P. Lawson]	To experience the dynamics of an alternate, unaccustomed role in a situation of community (or organization) conflict. To develop skills in conflict resolution, negotiation, and problem solving. To introduce process analysis and feedback as necessary community (or organization) development techniques.	A minimum of two hours	III-100

Awareness/Diagnosis (Continued)

Number	Title [Author]	Goals	Time Required	Volume & Page No.
82	**Greeting Cards:** An Organization Simulation	To observe a group's organizational style and functioning. To gather data on individuals' responses to creating and operating a production-centered organization. To give group members feedback on their organizational behavior.	Three to six hours	'72-44
98	**Strategies of Changing:** A Multiple-Role-Play [D.J. Marion & A. Edelman; *based on R. Chin & K.D. Benne*]	To acquaint people with three different interpersonal strategies for trying to effect change in human systems.	Approximately one hour	'73-32
131	**Roxboro Electric Company:** An OD Role-Play [H. Thomson, with B. Bell, M. Brosseau, P. Fleck, & F. Kahn]	To provide an experience in sensing organizational problems. To provide feedback on interviewing effectiveness. To explore organizational diagnosis and action planning.	Approximately two and one-half hours	'74-24
163	**Coloring Book:** An Organization Experiment [*based on M.J. Miller*]	To explore relationships between organizational design and task complexity.	Approximately one and one half hours	V-85
188	**Tug O'War:** A Force-Field Psychodrama [G. Friedrich]	To demonstrate the dynamics in a force-field analysis of a change situation. To involve participants in a problem-solving process.	Approximately one hour; one-half hour minimum; repetition with additional problems could take two hours	'77-22
193	**Tri-State:** A Multiple Role Play [H. Karp]	To build skills in diagnosing organizational and group problems. To focus attention on the interrelation between content and process issues.	Approximately two and one-half hours	'77-39

Awareness/Diagnosis (Continued)

Number	Title [Author]	Goals	Time Required	Volume & Page No.
194	**Top Secret Contract:** Intergroup Model Building [R.W. Landies & T. Isgar]	To provide a developing or an intact team an experience in the use of newly acquired skills in leadership style, problem solving, decision making, and communication processes. To study group dynamics in a task situation: competition/ collaboration, negotiation, confrontation/avoidance, etc. To point out the effect that external influences (outside agents, competition built into the system, production requirements, time and other constraints, etc.) have on team task accomplishment and on individual team members.	Approximately two and one-half hours	'77-47
228	**Homesell:** Intergroup Competition [J. Zimmerman]	To explore the ways in which members interact in a work group. To demonstrate different methods of group problem solving. To relate members' group behavior to back-home situations.	Approximately three hours. (May be conducted in two sessions of one and one-half hours each)	'78-46
325	**Meetings Audit:** Planning for Improvement [H.K. Baker]	To practice group planning and problem solving. To provide an opportunity for the members of an intact group to provide feedback about their meetings. To generate commitment to specific suggestions for improving the meetings of an intact group.	Two hours	'82-49

Awareness/Diagnosis (Continued)

Number	Title [Author]	Goals	Time Required	Volume & Page No.
347	**Elm Street Community Church:** Third-Party Consultation [C.E. List]	To provide the participants with an experience that simulates collaborative problem solving within an organization. To develop the participants' understanding of the role of a process consultant. To build skills in diagnosing organizational and group problems.	Approximately three hours	IX-34
348	**Inquiries:** Observing and Building Hypotheses [S.E. Aufrecht]	To provide the participants with experience in discovering relationships and meanings in an unfamiliar situation. To help the participants to become aware of their own methods of observing, gathering data, and building hypotheses. To allow the participants an opportunity to test the validity of these methods.	One and one-half hours	IX-48
351	**Team Planning:** Effects of Differential Information [T.J. Mallinson, R. Sept, & A. Tolliday]	To explore the dynamics of team planning. To examine the differences in communication, planning, and collaborative behavior when teams are given different amounts of information as the basis for completing a task.	Approximately two hours	IX-74
360	**Matrix:** Balancing Organizational Needs [J.P. Lewis]	To allow the participants to become acquainted with and experience a matrix organizational structure. To demonstrate the rewards and difficulties experienced by a group that concentrates on task and process simultaneously.	Approximately two hours	IX-136

Awareness/Diagnosis (Continued)

Number	Title [Author]	Goals	Time Required	Volume & Page No.
371	**Constructive Discipline:** Following Organizational Guidelines [A.J. Schuh]	To help the participants to develop an understanding of the importance and complexity of discipline problems within an organization. To develop the participants' awareness of the guidelines that can be used to handle discipline problems.	Approximately two hours	'84-49
372	**The Shoe-Distribution Company:** Exploring the Impact of Organizational Roles [M.A. Silverman]	To explore organizational dynamics. To help the participants to identify motivating forces within different organizational roles. To provide an opportunity for the participants to observe competition and/or collaboration as a result of organizational dynamics and roles.	Approximately two and one-half hours	'84-55
385	**Measuring Excellence:** Applying the Lessons of Peters and Waterman [L.D. Goodstein]	To help managers within an organization to identify their organization's degree of excellence. To develop a sense of cohesiveness and teamwork within management groups. To heighten the participants' awareness of existing management attitudes and practices within their organization. To enhance the participants' commitment to organizational excellence.	Approximately three and one-half hours	'85-81

Awareness/Diagnosis (Continued)

Number	Title [Author]	Goals	Time Required	Volume & Page No.
433	**Quantity Versus Quality:** Matching Perceptions of Performance [A.J. Schuh]	To enable managers to compare their perceptions with those of peers regarding the way each of them views the relative importance of quantity and quality in productivity. To help managers assess the accuracy and consistency of their individual perceptions by determining how closely they align with the perceptions of their peers.	One to one and one-half hours	'87-69
446	**Dos and Don'ts:** Developing Guidelines for Change [H.H. Johnson]	To enable the participants to identify their reactions to change in organizations. To assist the participants in developing guidelines for suggesting and implementing change in organizations.	Approximately two hours	'88-77
458	**The Impact Wheel:** An Empowerment Experience [B. Searle]	To help the participants to see ways in which they can empower themselves to affect their work lives. To provide the participants with a useful tool for identifying the effects and ramifications of events in their work lives. To offer the participants and opportunity to use this tool to analyze a particular work-related event.	Approximately one hour and forty-five minutes to two hours, depending on the number of subgroups	'89-83

Awareness/Diagnosis (Continued)

Number	Title [Author]	Goals	Time Required	Volume & Page No.
459	**The Robotics Decision:** Solving Strategic Problems [C.H. Smith]	To introduce the participants to the strategic assumption surfacing and testing (SAST) process as a tool for solving complex strategic problems. To offer the participants an opportunity to use the SAST process in solving a sample problem.	Approximately three and one-half hours	'89-89
484	**Metaphors:** Characterizing the Organization [J.W. Pfeiffer]	To offer the participants a way to clarify and discuss their perceptions of their organization. To allow the participants to compare their perceptions of an ideal organization with their perceptions of their own organization. To provide the participants with a means for analyzing their organization as they perceive it and for determining specific organizational changes that they would like to make.	Two hours to two hours and fifteen minutes	'91-125

Team Building

Number	Title [Author]	Goals	Time Required	Volume & Page No.
33	**Hollow Square:** A Communications Experiment [W.H. Schmidt & A. Shedlin]	To study dynamics involved in planning a task to be carried out by others. To study dynamics involved in accomplishing a task planned by others. To explore both helpful and hindering communication behaviors in assigning and carrying out a task.	Approximately one hour	II-32

Team Building (Continued)

Number	Title [Author]	Goals	Time Required	Volume & Page No.
68	**Intergroup Meeting:** An Image Exchange	To improve the relationship between two groups such as levels of management, majority-minority groups, males and females. To explore how groups interact with each other.	Three hours	III-81
160	**Tinkertoy® Bridge:** Intergroup Competition [G. Bellman]	To analyze individual and team actions in relation to on-the-job experiences. To build awareness of the need for teamwork in completing a task. To demonstrate the effects of competition on team efforts.	Approximately one and one-half hours	V-60
166	**Agenda Setting:** A Team-Building Starter [J.E. Jones]	To create and rank-order an agenda for a team-building session. To generate ownership of and commitment to commonly perceived problems facing a work group. To develop effective listening skills.	Approximately one hour	V-108
171	**Role Clarification:** A Team-Building Activity [J.E. Jones]	To clarify both expectations that team members have of others' roles and conceptions that team members have of their own roles. To promote renegotiation of role responsibilities within a work unit. To teach a process of role adjustment that can become a work group norm.	A minimum of three hours	V-136

Team Building (Continued)

Number	Title [Author]	Goals	Time Required	Volume & Page No.
232	**MANDOERS:** Organizational Clarification [T.H. Patten, Jr.]	To enable groups undergoing team-building efforts within the same organization to examine management and employee development organizational effectiveness, and reward systems in the work organization. To explore the diversity of views among participants regarding complex social and behavioral phenomena. To examine feelings resulting from organizational problems and to identify corrective actions that can be taken to deal with them.	Two to two and one-half hours	'78-71
289	**Intergroup Clearing:** A Relationship Building Intervention [L.C. Porter]	To "clear the air" between two work groups (departments, division, units, teams). To develop intergroup understanding and acceptance. To create the basis for an improved relationship between groups.	Approximately three hours	'81-48
297	**Group Effectiveness:** A Team-Building Activity [J.E. Jones & A.J. Reilly]	To increase team members' understanding of the concepts of group effectiveness. To generate commitment within an intact group to identify its interaction dynamics.	Approximately two hours	VIII-18

Team Building (Continued)

Number	Title [Author]	Goals	Time Required	Volume & Page No.
322	**Chips:** Agenda Building [C.A. Hill, Jr., & E.L. Emerson]	To select agenda items that have the highest value to the members of an intact group. To promote awareness of the agenda items of others and the degree of commitment to those items. To promote synergy in the group by means of negotiation.	One and one-half to two hours, plus prework	'82-31
327	**Work-Group Review:** Team Building [A.J. Schuh]	To provide an opportunity for open communication in an intact work group. To stimulate discussion between co-workers in the same work setting. To heighten awareness of co-workers' attitudes about work-related topics. To identify topics of concern collaboratively for further consideration and review by the organization.	Four and one-half hours, plus prework	'82-60
373	**Threats to the Project:** A Team-Building Activity [D.T. Simpson]	To increase the participants' understanding of group dynamics. To enhance the participants' effectiveness as team members.	Approximately one hour and forty-five minutes	'84-62
386	**Sharing and Supporting Goals:** A Team-Building Activity [R.L. Bunning]	To enhance the team-building process through self-disclosure, feedback, and interpersonal commitment. To offer the team members an opportunity to give and receive feedback about work-related, personal-growth goals. To develop the team members' commitment to support one another's growth goals.	One hour and forty-five minutes to four hours and fifteen minutes	'85-87

Team Building (Continued)

Number	Title [Author]	Goals	Time Required	Volume & Page No.
408	**Kaleidoscope:** Team Building Through Role Expansion [C.E. Cetti & M.K. Craig]	To allow members of a team to clarify their roles and to give and receive feedback about their existing and potential contributions to the team. To promote team building through self-disclosure, feedback, and commitment among team members. To widen the team members' views of one another's abilities and valuable qualities.	Two hours and twenty minutes to approximately six hours	X-122
409	**Sharing Perspectives:** Exchanging Views on Managerial and Worker Attitudes	To explore the origins of certain managerial and worker attitudes. To allow the participants to share and discuss their personal feelings about these attitudes. To help a manager and his or her subordinates to develop a greater understanding of one another so that their relationships can be improved in the future.	Approximately two hours	X-126

Team Building (Continued)

Number	Title [Author]	Goals	Time Required	Volume & Page No.
434	**Instant Survey:** Creating Agenda for Team Building [C.S. Cotton]	To generate working agenda for a meeting in which the participants will discuss their concerns about work-group issues that will face them in the future. To determine in a nonthreatening way the hidden needs and concerns of the participants. To present for discussion the concerns of all the participants. To provide participants with a method for creating participant-owned, meaningful agenda that will assist facilitators in designing team-building sessions for the participants.	From one and one-half to two hours	'87-75

Decision Making/Action Planning

Number	Title [Author]	Goals	Time Required	Volume & Page No.
132	**Planning Recommendations or Action:** A Team-Development Guidebook [R.P. Crosby]	To study the process of group decision making. To explore action planning.	Approximately three hours	'74-32
244	**What's Important on My Job?:** An Organization Development Activity [D.T. Simpson]	To examine perceptions about sources of motivation in work situations. To experience decision making by group consensus.	One and one-half hours. Additional facilitator time is required to conduct a pre-experience survey and tabulate the results	'79-71

Decision Making/Action Planning (Continued)

Number	Title [Author]	Goals	Time Required	Volume & Page No.
259	**Dhabi Fehru:** An MBO Activity [D. Bechtel]	To examine the process of developing task goals for individuals who are working together on a team project. To provide participants an opportunity to practice writing objectives as part of a Management by Objectives training session. To experience the difference between preparing goals for oneself and for others.	Three hours	VII-91
275	**Missiles:** Sources of Stress [K.A. Seger]	To identify sources of psychological stress. To demonstrate the effect that individual perceptions of situations have on behavior and decision making under stress. To experience the effects of various types of role power on persons in a decision-making situation.	Approximately two hours	'80-43
304	**When To Delegate:** A Manager's Dilemma [T.F. Carney]	To provide an opportunity to exchange views on the topic of delegation. To increase awareness of attitudes about task delegation.	Two and one-half to three hours	VIII-52
328	**Reviewing Objectives and Strategies:** A Planning Task for Managers [C.R. Mill]	To review and evaluate an organization's accomplish-ment of the past year. To clarify and reaffirm the organizational mission. To prepare objectives and action steps for major organizational efforts in the next year.	Approximately three hours	'82-65

Decision Making/Action Planning (Continued)

Number	Title [Author]	Goals	Time Required	Volume & Page No.
334	**Robbery:** Planning with PERT [M.P. Sharfman & T.R. Walters]	To illustrate the use of the Program Evaluation and Review Technique (PERT) and Critical Path Method (CPM) in planning. To allow participants to experience the scheduling and timing of both simultaneous and sequential activities. To demonstrate the creation of a basic PERT chart.	One and one-half to two hours	'83-40
336	**Vice President's In-Basket:** A Management Activity [A.N. Shelby]	To focus attention on the issues involved in setting priorities for communications in organizations. To increase awareness of the role of delegation in organizations.	Approximately three and one-half hours	'83-49
422	**Raises:** Evaluating Employee Performance [A.J. Schuh]	To provide participants with experience in considering qualifications for salary increases. To generate interest in and understanding of the importance and complexity of issues regarding salary increases.	Approximately two hours	'86-65
423	**Bars:** Developing Behaviorally Anchored Rating Scales [D.L. Farrow & J.A. Sample]	To collaboratively construct behaviorally anchored rating scales (BARS) for the relevant dimensions of a specific job position. To develop an example of a behaviorally based system of performance measurement.	Approximately three hours and forty minutes. (Varies depending on the size of the group)	'86-73

Decision Making/Action Planning (Continued)

Number	Title [Author]	Goals	Time Required	Volume & Page No.
447	**Delegation:** Using Time and Resources Effectively [M.N. O'Malley & C.M.T. Lombardozzi]	To assist the participants in identifying barriers to delegation, the benefits of delegation, and which kinds of tasks can be delegated and which cannot. To present the participants with a method for delegating. To provide the participants with an opportunity to practice planning delegation in accordance with this method.	Approximately two hours and fifteen minutes	'88-81

Conflict Resolution/Values

Number	Title [Author]	Goals	Time Required	Volume & Page No.
144	**Lindell-Billings Corporation:** A Confrontation Role-Play [T.H. Patten, Jr.]	To provide an opportunity to practice confrontation. To explore design considerations in using confrontation inside an organization. To examine and develop skills in intergroup conflict, negotiation, and problem solving.	Approximately three hours	'75-46
186	**Conflict Styles:** Organizational Decision Making [D.T. Simpson based on format by A. Zoll]	To identify ways of dealing with organizational or group conflict. To discuss when and why different methods of resolving conflict are appropriate to different situations. To provide an experience in group decision making.	Approximately one and one-half hours	'77-15

Conflict Resolution/Values (Continued)

Number	Title [Author]	Goals	Time Required	Volume & Page No.
268	**Sexual Values in Organizations:** An OD Role Play [P. Morrison]	To identify a range of personal, ethical, professional, and organizational considerations related to sexual relationships that occur between members of an organization. To determine the effect of such relationships on individual as well as organizational effectiveness.	Three hours	VII-146
339	**Organizational Blasphemies:** Clarifying Values [T. McNulty]	To provide an opportunity for the participants to be creatively open about aspects of their organizations. To identify and compare the organizational values of group members. To provide an opportunity to explore the match between the goals or values of the participants and those of the organization.	One to one and one-half hours	'83-77
340	**Conflict Role Play:** Resolving Differences [R.P. Belforti, L.A. Hagan, B. Markens, C.A. Monyak, G.N. Powell, & K.S. Sighinolfi]	To examine individuals' reactions to situations in which a "double standard" of behavior operates. To allow participants to explore their emotional responses to conflict. To examine the problem-solving behavior of participants in conflict situations in which a power difference exists.	Approximately two hours	'83-80

Conflict Resolution/Values (Continued)

Number	Title [Author]	Goals	Time Required	Volume & Page No.
374	**Trouble in Manufacturing:** Managing Interpersonal Conflict [J.E. Oliver]	To examine ways of managing interpersonal conflict in an organizational setting. To provide the participants with an opportunity to practice conflict management.	Approximately one and one-half hours	'84-67
375	**Datatrak:** Dealing with Organizational Conflict [D.J. Foscue & K.L. Murrell]	To illustrate the types of conflict that can arise within a work group. To provide the participants with an opportunity to experience and deal with organizational conflict. To help the participants to identify effective and ineffective methods of resolving conflict.	Two to two and one-half hours	'84-74
410	**The People of Trion:** Exploring Organizational Values [B.J. Allen, Jr.]	To offer the participants an opportunity to examine their organizational values. To explore the implications of the participants' organizational values. To explore the implications of differences between personal and organizational values. To examine the ways in which people are taught organizational values.	Approximately two hours	X-132
411	**The Gold Watch:** Balancing Personal and Professional Values [M.R. Lavery]	To provide an opportunity for the participants to examine, identify, and clarify their personal and professional values. To allow the participants to explore the interrelationship of personal values and values expressed by and in organizations.	Two hours	X-142

Conflict Resolution/Values (Continued)

Number	Title [Author]	Goals	Time Required	Volume & Page No.
472	**Termination:** Values and Decision Making [L.W. Sanders]	To offer the participants the opportunity to explore the impact of their values on individual and group decision making. To develop the participants' awareness of the need to identify objectives and to obtain sufficient information in group decision making. To provide the participants with an experience in group decision making.	One and one-half hours	'90-103
493	**Working at Our Company:** Clarifying Organizational Values [L.D. Goodstein]	To offer the participants an opportunity to examine and to discuss their personal and organizational values. To encourage the participants to explore the interaction of personal and organizational values. To enhance the participants' effectiveness as team members.	Approximately two hours	'92-79

Consultation Skills

Number	Title [Author]	Goals	Time Required	Volume & Page No.
34	**Hampshire In-Basket:** A Management Activity [J.W. Pfeiffer]	To discover general management principles through personal involvement with problem solving. To examine one's management style. To plan applications of management principles.	Approximately three hours	II-41
183	**Consulting Triads:** Self-Assessment [A.G. Banet, Jr.]	To assess consultation skills. To provide practice in one-to-one consultation.	Approximately two hours	'76-53

Consultation Skills (Continued)

Number	Title [Author]	Goals	Time Required	Volume & Page No.
211	**HELPCO:** An OD Role Play [N.E. Rand]	To study the processes of organization development (OD) consultation. To develop OD diagnosis, consultation, and observation skills.	Approximately three hours	VI-66
230	**Willington:** An Intervention-Skills Role Play [W.A. Randolph, J.C. Ferrie, & D.D. Palmer]	To determine the appropriate intervention strategy for a simulated organization. To implement a strategy for entering, initially diagnosing, and contracting with the simulated organization. To provide feedback on the consulting team members' interventions skills and strategy. To explore theory, skills, values, and strategies of organization development (OD).	Two and one-half to three hours	'78-55
. 424	**The Client-Consultant Questionnaire:** Checking for Client Involvement in OD [A.C. Ballew]	To present a way of determining whether a client really is involved in or committed to an organization development effort. To acquaint the participants with potential differences in diagnoses, values, and needs between a consultant and a client. To explore the potential for collusion for power and influence between the client and the consultant.	One and one-half to two hours	'86-79
435	**Winterset High School:** An Intergroup-Conflict Simulation [C.E. List]	To provide participants with an opportunity to practice a conflict-management strategy. To examine ways that occupational stereotyping can contribute to organizational conflict.	Approximately two and one-half hours	'87-79

Consultation Skills (Continued)

Number	Title [Author]	Goals	Time Required	Volume & Page No.
460	**City of Buffington:** Developing Consultation Skills [W.M. Bruce]	To provide the participants with an experience in diagnosing organizational problems. To offer the participants an opportunity to practice interviewing for the purpose of obtaining information for diagnosing organizational problems. To allow the participants to practice giving and receiving feedback on consulting skills used during data-gathering interviews.	Approximately two hours and fifteen to thirty minutes	'89-101
494	**Help Wanted:** Collaborative Problem Solving for Consultants [C. Nolde]	To offer the participants an opportunity to practice collaborative problem solving in one-on-one consulting situations and to receive feedback on their efforts. To assist the participants in identifying which consultant behaviors are effective in collaborative problem solving and which are not effective.	Approximately two and one-half hours	'92-87

FACILITATING LEARNING

Getting Acquainted

Number	Title [Author]	Goals	Time Required	Volume & Page No.
1	**Listening and Inferring:** A Getting-Acquainted Activity	To facilitate the involvement of individuals in a newly formed group.	Fifteen minutes	I-3
5	**Who Am I?:** A Getting-Acquainted Activity	To allow participants to become acquainted quickly in a relatively nonthreatening way.	Approximately forty-five minutes	I-19

Getting Acquainted (Continued)

Number	Title [Author]	Goals	Time Required	Volume & Page No.
49	**"Who Am I?"** **Variations:** A Getting-Acquainted Activity	To allow participants to become acquainted quickly in a non-threatening way.	Approximately forty-five minutes	III-3
101	**Getting Acquainted:** A Potpourri	To be used as ice breakers in human relations training events.	Varies with each listed experience	IV-3
245	**Tea Party:** An Ice Breaker [D. Keyworth]	To allow participants to share experiences and perceptions in a non-threatening manner. To promote acquaintance and a feeling of interaction in a new group.	Fifteen minutes to one hour	VII-5
269	**Autographs:** An Ice Breaker [J.E. Jones]	To facilitate the getting-acquainted process in a large group. To alleviate anxiety experienced during the beginning of a training session.	Approximately one-half hour	'80-11
281	**Alliterative Names:** A Getting-Acquainted Activity	To facilitate the getting-acquainted process in a small group. To promote self-disclosure in a new group.	Approximately one-half hour	'81-9
282	**Birth Signs:** An Ice Breaker [J.E. Jones]	To facilitate the getting-acquainted process in a large group. To alleviate participants' anxiety at the beginning of a training session.	Approximately one-half hour	'81-11
293	**Name Tags:** An Ice Breaker [D. Marting & C. Cherrey]	To provide participants with an opportunity to introduce themselves in a nonthreatening and enjoyable manner. To develop an atmosphere conducive to group interaction.	Fifteen minutes	VIII-5

Getting Acquainted (Continued)

Number	Title [Author]	Goals	Time Required	Volume & Page No.
294	**Learning Exchange:** A Getting-Acquainted Activity [A.F. Farquharson]	To provide an opportunity for participants to get to know each other. To demonstrate the knowledge and skills that the participants have brought to the group. To raise awareness of factors that enhance the teaching-learning process.	Approximately one hour	VIII-7
295	**People on the Job:** Expressing Opinions [M.B. Ross]	To afford participants the opportunity to share their views in a structured environment. To provide a sense of the variety of opinions and attitudes that exist about a particular subject. To develop a climate for future group interaction.	One and one-half to two hours	VIII-10
317	**Rebus Names:** Getting Acquainted [A.D. Toppins]	To facilitate the getting-acquainted process among members of a new group. To facilitate the involvement and interaction of individuals in a newly formed group.	One hour	'82-9
329	**Just the Facts:** Getting Acquainted [R.N. Glenn]	To provide an opportunity for members of a group to become acquainted with one another in a non-threatening manner. To create an atmosphere conducive to group interaction and sharing.	One to one and one-half hours	'83-11

Getting Acquainted (Continued)

Number	Title [Author]	Goals	Time Required	Volume & Page No.
376	**Group Savings Bank:** An Introductory Experience [D. Libkind & D.M. Dennis]	To help the participants to become acquainted with one another. To develop the participants' readiness for involvement at the beginning of a group session. To provide the participants with an opportunity to experiment with abandoning old behaviors and/or adopting new behaviors.	Approximately forty-five minutes	'84-92
436	**I Represent:** A World Meeting [P. Doyle]	To facilitate the getting-acquainted process. To enable participants to express indirectly how they would like to be perceived.	One to one and one-half hours	'87-87

Forming Subgroups

Number	Title [Author]	Goals	Time Required	Volume & Page No.
2	**Two-Four-Eight:** Building Teams	To divide a large group into workable subgroups in such a way as to increase group cohesiveness and identity.	Approximately thirty minutes	I-5
27	**Jigsaw:** Forming Groups	To establish group cohesion by forming a large number of participants into groups with pre-determined compositions.	Approximately thirty minutes	II-10
51	**Empty Chair:** An Extended Group Design	To allow all participants to become involved voluntarily in a group-on-group experience when the size of the total group makes discussion impractical.	Open	III-8

Forming Subgroups (Continued)

Number	Title [Author]	Goals	Time Required	Volume & Page No.
125	**Hum-Dinger:** A Getting-Acquainted Activity [A.D. Duncan]	To break a large group into smaller groups in a nonthreatening manner. To facilitate contact between all members of a large group in a related climate of fun and humor.	Approximately thirty minutes	'74-7
173	**Limericks:** Getting Acquainted [E. Racicot]	To acquaint and involve participants with one another through non-threatening physical activity. To divide a large group into subgroups in a climate of humor and cohesiveness.	Approximately thirty minutes	'76-7
387	**Daffodil:** Getting Acquainted in Small Groups [M.D. Laus]	To assemble the participants into small groups in a nonthreatening manner. To facilitate the getting acquainted process by generating contact among the participants.	Approximately forty-five minutes	'85-91

Expectations of Learners/Facilitators

Number	Title [Author]	Goals	Time Required	Volume & Page No.
91	**Perception of Task:** A Teaching-Learning Exercise [R.T. Williams]	To examine how perceptions of a learning task by teacher and learner influence teaching styles and learning styles.	One hour	'73-15
96	**Participants-Staff Expectations** [A.H. Munoz]	To provide participants and facilitators the opportunity to examine and discuss mutual expectations and perceptions regarding the training program. To reduce the "expectation gap" between participants and facilitators.	Approximately one hour	'73-29

Expectations of Learners/Facilitators (Continued)

Number	Title [Author]	Goals	Time Required	Volume & Page No.
324	**Needs, Expectations, and Resources:** Beginning a Workshop [J. Goodman & J.A. Bellanca]	To allow participants in a long-term training workshop to become acquainted with one another. To identify and clarify the needs, expectations, and resources of the group facilitator and the participants in a long-term training workshop. To establish a cooperative, nonthreatening climate in the workshop group.	One and one-half to two hours	'82-46
412	**Client Concerns:** Developing Appropriate Trainer Responses	To develop the participants' skills in devising appropriate responses to representative client statements. To offer the participants an opportunity to explore ways of handling various client concerns and expectations. To help the participants to identify their individual biases about various training issues.	One hour and forty-five minutes	X-148

Dealing with Blocks to Learning

Number	Title [Author]	Goals	Time Required	Volume & Page No.
42	**First Names, First Impressions:** A Feedback Experience [J.E. Jones]	To get acquainted with other members of a small group. To discover one's initial impact on others. To study phenomena related to first impressions-their accuracy and effects.	Approximately one hour	II-88
43	**Verbal Activities Within Groups:** A Potpourri	To be used as openers when meetings of the groups are infrequent, or may be used as interventions within meetings.	Varies with each activity	II-91

Dealing with Blocks to Learning (Continued)

Number	Title [Author]	Goals	Time Required	Volume & Page No.
87	**Peter-Paul:** Getting Acquainted [E.L. Solley]	To help group members get acquainted quickly in a relatively nonthreatening manner. To explore feelings generated by "becoming another person." To explore the dimensions of a brief encounter. To emphasize the need for careful, active listening during conversation.	Minimum of ten minutes plus two minutes per group member	'73-7
89	**Gunnysack:** An Introduction to Here-and-Now [J.E. Jones]	To establish the norm of attending to here-and-now data and "gunny-sacking" then-and-there data. To help participants to become aware of their own here-and-now reactions.	Approximately thirty minutes	'73-11
106	**Sculpturing:** An Expression of Feelings [L.A. McKeown, B.Kaye, R, McLean, & I. Linhardt]	To provide a nonverbal medium for the expression of feelings toward another person. To promote feedback on individual behavior.	Approximately forty-five minutes	IV-21
112	**The "T" Test:** An Experiential Lecture on Traits [A.J. Reilly]	To introduce the concept of personality traits. To illustrate the process of inferring characteristics from behavior. To help diminish some of the unproductive anxiety which is often associated with filling out psychological instruments or inventories.	Approximately thirty minutes	IV-41
145	**Win What, Lose What?:** An Intergroup Conflict Intervention [K. Finn]	To examine the elements of intergroup conflict. To illustrate a process of conflict resolution.	Approximately three hours	'75-51

Dealing with Blocks to Learning (Continued)

Number	Title [Author]	Goals	Time Required	Volume & Page No.
191	**Communication Analysis:** A Getting-Acquainted Activity [R.D. Jorgenson]	To establish a laboratory-learning climate in the initial stages of a group composed of hostile or reluctant participants. To experience openness in exploring positive and negative feelings in a non-threatening atmosphere. To examine how affective elements, especially negative feelings, influence the result of communication.	Approximately one hour	'77-32
301	**Resistance to Learning:** Developing New Skills [H. Bracey & R. Trueblood]	To provide a model for understanding the phenomenon of behavioral resistance in learning situations. To demonstrate various behavioral manifestations of resistance. To increase awareness of techniques that can be used to overcome resistance in learning situations.	Two hours	VIII-37
342	**News Bulletin:** Focusing the Group [F.E. Woodall]	To develop readiness for interaction at the beginning of a group session. To free group members from personal concerns so that they can concentrate on group matters.	Approximately five minutes per member	IX-8

Building Trust

Number	Title [Author]	Goals	Time Required	Volume & Page No.
45	**Helping Pairs:** A Collection	To build helping relationships ancillary to small-group experiences. To give participants an opportunity to try out new behavior within a dyadic relationship. To provide group members with ways of checking out heir perceptions of and reactions to laboratory experiences.	Varies with each activity	II-97
90	**Make Your Own Bag:** Symbolic Self-Disclosure [C. Lawson]	To raise levels of trust and openness in a group. To make group members aware of themselves and others as persons.	Approximately one hour and forty-five minutes	'73-13
120	**Dimensions of Trust:** A Symbolic Expression [J. Costigan]	To explore the various dimensions and meanings of trust. To promote the creative expression of trust.	Approximately one hour	IV-96
196	**Current Status:** A Feedback Activity on Trust [R.N. Glenn]	To examine unexpressed feelings of trust or distrust within an ongoing group and to clarify the reasons for these feelings of trust within the group. To promote self-disclosure and risk taking. To provide a basis for subsequent assessment of group trust.	Approximately one and one-half hours	'77-57

Building Norms of Openness

Number	Title [Author]	Goals	Time Required	Volume & Page No.
25	**Group Conversation:** Discussion-Starters [D. Castle]	To develop a compatible climate and readiness for interaction in a group through sharing personal experience.	Can be a fifteen-minute preface to other group activities or planned for an entire meeting	II-3
88	**"Cold" Introductions:** Getting Acquainted [J.E. Jones]	To help participants to get to know each other while building expectations of risk taking and receptivity to feedback. To build norms of openness, experimentation, and attention to process.	Approximately three minutes per participant	'73-9
93	**Building Open and Closed Relationships** *[adapted from W. Barber]*	To enable group members to focus on the elements of relationships which characterize them as open or closed. To facilitate the cohesiveness of personal growth or otherwise-designated group who will be working together.	One and one-half to two hours	'73-20

Building Norms of Openness (Continued)

Number	Title [Author]	Goals	Time Required	Volume & Page No.
109	**Growth Cards:** Experimenting with New Behavior [M. Cahn]	To develop an accepting atmosphere for risk taking and self-disclosure. To give those within a larger laboratory community a legitimate entry point for the provision of individual feedback to participants in other groups. To supply participants with specific, individual feedback to aid them in making decisions concerning an agenda for modifying their own behavior. To increase understanding and acceptance of personality components which decrease interpersonal effectiveness. To strengthen individual commitment to behavioral change through open verbalization and the development of a method or prescription for modification. To reinforce group skills of decision making and task performance.	Approximately two hours	IV-30
129	**Forced-Choice Identity:** A Self-Disclosure Activity [J.J. Sherwood]	To gain insight about oneself. To facilitate self-disclosure and feedback. To encourage community building. To enhance enjoyment of the group experience through a change-of-pace activity.	Approximately two hours	'74-20
174	**Labeling:** A Getting Acquainted Activity [C.L. Kormanski]	To provide opportunities to become acquainted with other members of the group. To promote feedback and self-disclosure among participants regarding initial perceptions.	Approximately one hour	'76-10

Building Norms of Openness (Continued)

Number	Title [Author]	Goals	Time Required	Volume & Page No.
197	**Best Friend:** A Getting-Acquainted Activity [D.L. Garris]	To afford participants the opportunity to introduce themselves in a non-threatening manner. To develop a climate for group interaction by sharing personal information.	Approximately forty-five minutes	VI-3
246	**Personal Identity:** An Ice Breaker [D.E. Whiteside]	To enable participants to 'try on' new identities. To explore the influence on the behavior of others. To explore the relationship between honesty and trust.	Approximately one hour	VII-11
448	**The Golden Egg Award:** Facilitating Openness [C.P. Alexander]	To assist the participants in building a group norm of openness. To promote self-disclosure and to develop the participants' ability to interact openly during group work. To enhance the participants' understanding of "mistakes" as opportunities for learning.	Approximately one hour and ten minutes	'88-89

Energizers

Number	Title [Author]	Goals	Time Required	Volume & Page No.
149	**Energizers:** Group Starters	To prepare participants for meetings	Varies with each activity	V-3

Evaluating Learning-Group Process

Number	Title [Author]	Goals	Time Required	Volume & Page No.
24	**Assumptions About Human Relations Training:** An Opinionnaire [J.E. Jones'; worksheets by J. Dickinson, C. Dee, J.E. Jones, & B.H. Arbes]	To allow the group to assess the degree to which it has consensus on a number of assumptions that underlie laboratory learning. To assist co-facilitators in identifying each other's biases about training. To discover some possible "blind spots" that the training staff may have about training.	Minimum of one hour	I-107
55	**Group Self-Evaluations:** A Collection of Instruments	To help a group evaluate its own functioning. To provide a way to examine objectively the participation of group members. To explore the norms that have developed in a group which has been meeting for some time.	Varies according to the evaluative procedures used	III-22
74	**Personal Journal:** A Self-Evaluation	To heighten participants' awareness of the sequence of events and the corresponding emotional development which takes place In a laboratory or a workshop. To aid in self disclosure.	Any number of periods of ten to fifteen minutes each, depending on the laboratory or workshop	III-109
85	**Growth and Name Fantasy** [A.G. Banet, Jr.]	To provide group participants with an opportunity to review, in fantasy, the phases of growth and development they have accomplished. To review their sense of individual identity.	Approximately forty-five minutes	'72-59

Evaluating Learning-Group Process (Continued)

Number	Title [Author]	Goals	Time Required	Volume & Page No.
92	**Medial Feedback:** A "Mid-Course" Correction Exercise	To generate evaluative data about the effects of a laboratory education design while there is still time to modify it. To study group process phenomena both as a participant and as an observer.	Approximately one and one-half hours	'73-17
182	**The Other You:** Awareness Expansion [A.J. Reilly]	To increase personal self-awareness. To provide participants an opportunity to experiment with new behavior. To help participants integrate new data into their self-concepts.	Approximately two and one-half hours	'76-51
214	**Roles Impact Feelings:** A Role Play [M. Smith]	To enable participants to become aware of some of the roles they play. To discover how roles product feelings.	Approximately two and one-half hours	VI-102
234	**Buttermilk:** Awareness Expansion [T.R. Harvey]	To demonstrate the processes of interpersonal influence and personal change. To "warm up" groups that are interested in exploring the dynamics of change.	One-half hour	'79-13

Evaluating Learning-Group Process (Continued)

Number	Title [Author]	Goals	Time Required	Volume & Page No.
388	**Smackers:** Group Mid-Life Assessment [R.L. Hughes]	To provide a mid-life assessment and growth experience for an intact group. To help the participants to identify behaviors and personal qualities that are valuable within a group. To allow the participants to give and receive feedback about the ways in which their behavior and personal qualities are perceived within the group. To develop the participants' ability and willingness to evaluate one anothers' behavior and personal qualities in the interest of improving group functioning.	Approximately two hours	'85-95

Developing Group Facilitator Skills

Number	Title [Author]	Goals	Time Required	Volume & Page No.
26	**Miniversity.** Sharing Participants' Ideas	To provide for dissemination of information, using participants as resources, during a conference, workshop, or institute.	Time is dependent on the size of the group, the facilities available, and the number of "courses" offered	II-7
47	**Microlab:** A Training Demonstration	To demonstrate human relations training methods. To accelerate the development of growth-producing norms, such as openness and attention to feelings.	Depends on variations employed in the design	II-113

Developing Group Facilitator Skills (Continued)

Number	Title [Author]	Goals	Time Required	Volume & Page No.
48	**Process Intervention:** A facilitator Practice Session	To provide practice in intervening in small groups. To generate feedback on intervention styles.	At least one hour	II-115
148	**Group Leadership Functions:** A Facilitator-Style Activity [R.K. Conyne]	To explore four basic leadership functions of group facilitators. To study the relationship between leadership functions and general interpersonal style.	Approximately two hours	'75-63
172	**Group Composition:** A Selection Activity [G.M. Phillips & A.G. Banet, Jr.]	To explore the process of selection of group members. To assist facilitators in identifying their biases about group composition. To study similarities and differences between personal growth and psychotherapy groups.	Approximately one and one-half hours	V-139
495	**Good Workshops Don't Just Happen:** Developing Facilitation Skills [K. Kreis]	To assist the participant in identifying elements of facilitation that are (1) vital to workshop effectiveness, (2) harmful to workshop effectiveness, and (3) reflective of style (rather that vital or harmful). To offer the participants an opportunity to consider and discuss facilitation practices, techniques, and styles.	Approximately two hours	'92-97

Developing Group Facilitator Skills (Continued)

Number	Title [Author]	Goals	Time Required	Volume & Page No.
496	**Up Close and Personal with Dr. Maslow:** Designing Training To Meet Trainees' Needs [B. Jameson]	To explore Abraham Maslow's (1970) theory of the hierarchy of needs as the basis for creating a positive learning climate in a training experience. To present a format for designing a training module. To offer the participants an opportunity to practice designing and presenting a training module that meets trainees' needs.	Approximately three hours	'92-111

Closure

Number	Title [Author]	Goals	Time Required	Volume & Page No.
86	**Symbolic Closing Exercise** [M. Smith]	To finish a workshop or laboratory with a sense of closure. To re-enact the group process in symbolic nonverbal action.	Approximately ten minutes	'72-61
114	**Closure.** Variations on a Theme	To be useful in closing human relations training events. Can also be employed to foster self-disclosure in personal growth groups.	Varies with each idea	IV-49
176	**Symbolic Toast:** A Closure Experience [A.D. Duncan & J.F. Dorris]	To provide closure at the end of a training experience. To provide an opportunity for participants to give and receive feedback. To allow each person to receive some personal validation from each member of the group. To affirm the personal strengths of the participants.	Approximately forty minutes	'76-17

Closure (Continued)

Number	Title [Author]	Goals	Time Required	Volume & Page No.
201	**Bread Making:** An Integrating Experience [A.G. Banet, Jr.]	To experience collaborating on an unusual group task. To focus on the sensory, fantasy, and creative aspects of food preparation. To provide a sensory, nonverbal background for integrating learning in the final stages of a workshop.	Approximately one hour and twenty minutes (One sixty-minute period followed by one twenty-minute period later on)	VI-19
222	**Golden Awards:** A Closure Activity [J. Elliott-Kemp & G. Williams]	To provide an opportunity for group and self-appraisal. To allow members a chance to see how others perceive them. To practice giving feedback to others in a constructive and helpful manner.	Approximately two hours	'78-12
318	**Kia Ora:** Closure [P.M. Swain]	To provide closure at the end of a training experience. To provide an opportunity for participants to express feelings generated by the group experience. To introduce aspects of Maori culture that pertain to interpersonal encounter.	Approximately thirty to forty-five minutes	'82-12

INTRODUCTION TO INSTRUMENTS

Instrumented survey-feedback tools (generally inventories or measurement scales) can be used in a number of ways by group facilitators. Data from inventories can be interpreted normatively or intrapersonally, but it is important that they be coordinated carefully with the goals of the training design. Some uses of instrumentation include the following:

Providing instrumented feedback to group members. Participants complete, score, and interpret their own scales. They can be asked to predict one another's scores. They can fill out scales for one another as feedback.

Manipulating group composition. For brief, experimental demonstrations of the effects of group composition, various mixes of group members can be established. Long-term groups can be built that offer the promise of beneficial outcomes. Extremes of both homogeneity and heterogeneity can be avoided.

Teaching theory of interpersonal functioning. Some brief instruments are intended primarily to introduce concepts. Participants are involved with theory by investing in an activity such as completing an inventory related to the model being explored.

Researching outcomes of training interventions. Even scales with relatively low reliability can be effective in the study of group phenomena when used with pretest or follow-up procedures.

Studying here-and-now process in groups. It is sometimes helpful to use an instrument to assist the group in diagnosing its own internal functioning. The data can be focused on what is happening and what changes are desirable.

DISADVANTAGES AND ADVANTAGES OF USING INSTRUMENTS[1]

It is important to note both the advantages and the disadvantages of using instruments in training.

Disadvantages

One of the key disadvantages of using instruments is that people often fear that someone has, so to speak, obtained an indelible fingerprinting of them, that they have been exposed, that somebody has read their minds. It is important for

---

[1]The following discussion on the disadvantages and advantages of using instruments is based on *Instrumentation in Human Relations Training* (2nd ed.) (pp. 11-17) by J.W. Pfeiffer, R. Heslin, and J.E. Jones, 1976, San Diego, CA: Pfeiffer & Company.

facilitators using instruments to reduce this tendency to overstate the accuracy and stability of an instrument.

Another disadvantage is that instruments tend to encourage participants to be dependent on the facilitator, thus locating the leadership (control) of the group with the facilitator rather than allowing it to be shared among the members.

The use of instruments can be a means of dissipating the useful tension of person-to-person encounter, especially in a personal growth workshop. Both the participants and the leader may be denied some of the ambiguous but potentially growth-inducing tension produced by face-to-face encounter and reactions to one another.

Instruments often generate a rash of nitpicking responses in which the participants question the items, reliability, validity, or relevance of an instrument. Much valuable time can be used in arguing about the instrument itself. Nitpicking often is a result of the fact that the participants have received information that disturbs them; they fear that their profiles *are* irrevocably them or that people are going to interpret their data in a negative fashion.

Instruments also have the potential to generate significant hostility from participants who may see them as irrelevant, time consuming, and, in general, diverting attention from the key issues of the workshop.

Finally, instruments can supply a person with more feedback than he or she is ready to handle; in other words, an instrument can overload participants with information that they do not have time to assimilate, to work through, and to put into perspective.

Avoiding the Disadvantages

A number of the disadvantages mentioned can be avoided by removing the mysticism surrounding instruments. Effort should be made to prevent people from assuming that an instrument is an error-free, God-directed opening of the soul to everyone. Rather, participants should be encouraged to view instrumented experiences like any other choice-making experience in their everyday lives. They have given answers to situations described in the instrument, added up those answers, and come up with scores. If they have trouble understanding where their scores came from, they should be encouraged to go back to each item fed into the score, examine how they responded to each item and how they scored it, and perhaps compare their responses to other people's—item by item, response by response, and situation by situation.

A second way to avoid some of the disadvantages of instruments is to make sure that individuals have sufficient time to process what the instrument has revealed about them. All participants should be given an opportunity to talk through their scores, to compare their scores in detail with those of others in the group, and to discuss why they see life from perspectives that are different from the perspectives of other participants. They may also discuss how their views of their scores reflect their personal orientations and may compare their views and orientations with those of other people.

Advantages

Instrumented approaches give the participants early opportunities to develop an understanding of the theories involved in the dynamics of their own group situations—understanding that will increase their involvement. By judiciously choosing an appropriate instrument during the first group session, the facilitator can quickly offer the participants a theory about personal styles or preferences, group or team development, interpersonal relations, or leadership that they can use throughout the rest of the group experience.

Another advantage of using instruments is that they give the participants some constructs and terminology early in the group experience that they can use in looking at their own and other people's behavior and in categorizing and describing what goes on between persons or within a person. A related advantage is that people form commitments to the information, constructs, and theory that they have been given, because their instrumented feedback describes them in terms of these constructs. One way of tying a person's ego to some useful theory about groups or interpersonal relations is to give the theory personal impact.

Another advantage is that participants can be given feedback about their personal behavior early in a group experience. Often in workshops, participants do not receive feedback about their styles or ways of relating to other participants until the last day, the last meeting, or the last two or three hours of the workshop. It may take that long before they have developed the skills necessary to give effective feedback and before an atmosphere of trust can be developed in the group so that members can feel comfortable in giving that kind of feedback to another member. Regardless of the causes of this situation, people then are faced with new information about themselves with no time to work on new behaviors that might modify those aspects described. Instruments administered early in the group experience help to compensate for the lack of feedback from others by giving each person some information about his or her style, perceptual framework toward other people, and reactions of others. Thus, people can generate agendas of behavior modification for themselves, based on the characteristics uncovered by the instrument, while they still have the remainder of the workshop to work on them.

Instruments surface latent issues that should be dealt with in the group setting. This is true whether the issues and problems are within an individual, between individuals, or within an organization. By administering an instrument that uncovers these issues, the facilitator makes these issues public, that is, outside the individual or the organization. These issues then become legitimate materials to deal with, to discuss, to try to correct, or to improve.

Instruments give feedback to an individual or an organization in a way that is characterized by relatively low threat. When a person receives information from a questionnaire that he or she personally has filled out, the person is more likely to trust those data than data received from another individual about his or her personal style. At least the person does not have the dilemma of trying to sort out whether the information is mostly a function of his or her behavior, of the perceptual framework of the person who is giving the feedback, or of some chemistry that exists between the two of them. People can be fairly sure that the instrument holds no personal malevolence toward them; therefore, they can be freer to accept the information, understanding the fact that the information actually came from their own responses to descriptions of situations.

Another advantage is that instruments not only give individualized feedback about the respondents, but also allow the respondents to compare themselves with others. We all are aware that we may be more or less dominating than other people, that we may enjoy being with people more or less than others, that we may have a greater or lesser need for people to like us, and so on. However, it is often an eye-opening experience to find out that we are stronger in one or more of our characteristics than 99 percent of the people in a certain norm group. This last piece of information, indicating that a person ranks not only high on a characteristic, but *unusually* high, may cause that person to pause and examine carefully whether this characteristic is becoming dysfunctional, for example, getting in the way of his or her performance on the job or at home.

Instruments allow the facilitator of a small group to focus the energies and time of the participants on the most appropriate material and also to control, to some extent, the matters that are dealt with in the workshop. In this way the facilitator is able to ensure that the issues worked on are crucial, existing ones rather than less important ones that the members may introduce to avoid grappling with the more uncomfortable issues.

A final advantage is that instruments allow longitudinal assessment of change in a group, an organization, or an individual. This assessment can be useful in organization development for demonstrating that the group interventions in which the organization is involved are compatible with the goals the consultant has determined from sensing efforts and/or compatible with the stated goals of the organization. This advantage is valuable in terms of group research and also for personal goal feedback.

SUMMARY

The Use of Instrumentation in Small Groups

Disadvantages

Engenders fear of exposure

Fosters dependency on the facilitator

Relieves tension that could lead to growth

Generates time-consuming nitpicking

May be seen as diverting from key issues and may arouse hostility

Can result in overload of feedback

Advantages

Enables early, easy theoretical learning

Develops early understanding of constructs and terminology

Produces personal commitment to information, theory, and constructs

Supplies early personal feedback

Surfaces latent issues

Fosters open reception of feedback through low threat

Provides for comparison of individuals with norm groups

Allows facilitator to focus and control group appropriately

Facilitates longitudinal assessment of change

Avoiding the Disadvantages of Instruments

1. The facilitator can make a concerned effort to remove the mysticism
   surrounding instrumentation:
   a. By discussing the margin of error and other factors that contribute to
      less-than-absolute results.
   b. By allowing and encouraging participants to explore the instrument
      thoroughly so that they see how it was designed and how their scores
      were derived.
   c. By showing participants how instrumentation is related to everyday,
      choice-making experiences.

2. The facilitator can ensure that sufficient time is made available for processing the data:

    a. By giving participants an opportunity to talk through their scores and to compare their scores with those of others.

    b. By emphasizing and legitimizing the differing life perspectives and orientations of people.

SEVEN PHASES IN USING AN INSTRUMENT

Using an instrument properly, that is, obtaining the best possible value from it, entails seven different phases: (1) administration, (2) theory input, (3) prediction, (4) scoring, (5) interpretation, (6) posting, and (7) processing.

In the first step, *administration,* a nonthreatening atmosphere should be established and the purposes of the instrument discussed. In larger groups, particularly, the administrator may need to tell those individuals who finish first to wait quietly for the others to finish.

Next, the facilitator should take a few minutes to give the participants some *theory input* for the instrument by explaining the rationale behind its use.

Each participant should be asked to make a *prediction* about his or her score(s) by estimating whether he or she will score high, medium, or low and by recording the estimate.

Scoring can be done in a number of ways. Some instruments require templates; some are self-scoring; and some require that scores be announced, written on newsprint, or handed out on a reproduced sheet. The sophistication of the particular group is a gauge of the most appropriate method of scoring. Sometimes it is more efficient for the facilitator or an assistant to do the scoring than to have participants do it. In this way, of course, individuals do not receive instant feedback, but often the instrument can be administered before a meal break and the results made available immediately after the break. The essential guideline in scoring is that it should not detract from the data being generated.

The manner in which *interpretation* is handled may vary widely, depending on the group and the style of the facilitator. One suggested way is to use two stages: (1) an interpretation of the administrator's (or another staff member's) scores, and then (2) an interpretation between pairs of participants. Thus, participants can first see how interpretations are made. Also, if staff members are willing to share their scores, participants find it less threatening to share theirs.

The sixth phase is *posting.* Displaying scores on newsprint can dissipate some people's concerns about possible negative values attached to their scores. At the same time, it can generate additional useful data for the group. Posting scores for discussion is particularly effective in subgroups.

The final, and perhaps most crucial, phase of instrumentation is *processing*. Group processing can simultaneously defuse negative affect and promote integration of the data concepts. Six to twelve participants form a group of ideal size for processing.

WHAT TO LOOK FOR IN AN INSTRUMENT

In examining the training applications and uses of instruments, we have identified some dimensions that need to be considered in selecting or assessing an instrument. The following chart reflects our judgment of the relative amount of concern each dimension warrants in training, organizational survey, personnel selection, and research applications.

INSTRUMENTATION APPLICATION

DIMENSION	Training	Organizational Assessment	Personnel Selection	Research
Validity* Are the data useful?	High	High	High	High
Reliability How accurate or stable are the scores?	Medium	Medium	Medium	High
Objectivity Is the scoring dependent on the judgments of the scorer, or is there a standard key?	High	High	High	Medium
Theoretical base Is the instrument based on a workable model?	High	High	Low	High

---

*Validity takes on different meanings in these four contexts. In *training* the validity of the scale is in the user; that is, "Can I use this scale to help participants in training learn more effective behavior?" In *organizational assessment* the overriding consideration is "Does this instrument tap those process dimensions that are correlated with production?" In *personnel selection* the use of instruments centers around predictive—or discriminative—validity: "Is this instrument significantly related to a meaningful success criterion?" In *research* the major concern is the theoretical constructs being measured: "Does this scale measure the concepts derived from theory sufficiently well to permit meaningful tests of hypothesis derived from the model used?" Validity is always situation-specific; it resides not so much in the instrument as in the particular use of it.

INSTRUMENTATION APPLICATION

DIMENSION	Training	Organizational Assessment	Personnel Selection	Research
Behavioral orientation Are the scores derived from the respondents' descriptions of their behavior?	High	High	Low	Low
Observability Can the scores be related to the observable behavior of respondents?	High	Medium	Low	Low
Language Is the instrument written at an appropriate reading level? Does it use a special vocabulary or jargon?	High	High	High	High
Special training How much professional preparation is required to use the scale?	High	High	High	High
Adaptability Can the items be adapted/ amended to fit a particular situation?	Medium	High	Low	Low
Copyright restrictions Can it be reprinted or edited without special permission?	High	Medium	Medium	Medium
Transparency How obvious is the rationale underlying the items?	Low	Low	High	Medium
Fakeability How easy is it for respondents to manipulate their scores?	Low	Medium	High	Medium
Norms Are relevant norms available?	Low	Low	High	Medium
Time required How much time is needed to prepare, administer, score, and interpret the instrument?	High	High	Low	Medium

INSTRUMENTATION APPLICATION

DIMENSION	Training	Organizational Assessment	Personnel Selection	Research
Expense What is the cost of the materials, scoring, analyses, and background documents? Are these reusable materials?	Medium	High	Medium	Medium
Accessibility Are the materials readily available?	Medium	Medium	Medium	Medium
Special materials Does the instrument require that any special apparatus be set up in advance?	High	Medium	Medium	Medium
Noxiousness Would the items—or the scale itself—offend intended respondents?	High	High	Medium	High
Scoring complexity Can the instrument be self-scored? Are electronic/clerical options available?	High	Low	Medium	Low
Data reduction How many scores are derived? Can these be summarized for ease in interpretation?	High	High	Medium	Low
Handouts Are easily read interpretive materials available to be distributed to respondents?	Medium	Medium	Low	Low
Familiarity How likely is it that participants will have responded to the scale before?	Low	Low	Medium	High

CLASSIFICATION OF INSTRUMENTS

With the publication of the 1984 *Annual,* we instituted a new policy regarding instruments. Since that time, the theoretical background necessary for understanding, presenting, and utilizing each instrument has been included with the instrument, as have been all forms, scoring sheets, and interpretive materials. Thus, all the materials (including any pertinent lecturette material) that the facilitator needs in order to use an instrument from this section of the 1984 through 1992 *Annuals* are included either directly before or directly after the instrument form itself.

In this edition of the *Reference Guide* (as in the 1990 edition), we have reclassified the instruments in order to help the user to find materials more quickly and with more discrimination. The instruments are classified according to what they *measure*—the focus of the information they provide, *not* according to how they might be used. The categories and subcategories are as follows:

> Communication
>
> Consulting/Facilitation
> > General
> > Training/Learning Style
>
> Groups/Teams
>
> Interpersonal
>
> Management/Leadership
> > General
> > Attitudes
>
> Organizations
> > Diagnosis
> > Employee Attitudes/Motivation
> > Values/Culture
>
> Personal
> > General
> > Conflict/Stress
> > Life Planning/Career Management
> > Values/Sexual Issues

COMMUNICATION

Title	Author(s)	Volume & Page No.
Feedback Rating Scales		III-28
Interpersonal Communication Inventory	M.J. Bienvenu, Sr.	'74-98
The Language System Diagnostic Instrument	C. Torres	'86-104

CONSULTING/FACILITATION
General

Title	Author(s)	Volume & Page No.
Helping Relationship Inventory	J.E. Jones; *adapted from* E.H. Porter	'73-55
Group Leadership Functions Scale	R.K. Conyne	'75-65
Critical Consulting Incidents Inventory (CCII)	J.E. Jones & A.G. Banet, Jr.	'78-91
The Group Incidents Questionnaire	J.P. Stokes & R.C. Tait	'81-77
Survey of Program Participants	R.M. Wolf & W.W. Burke	'82-91
Follow-Up Survey of Program Participants	R.M. Wolf & W.W. Burke	'82-98
Training Philosophies Profile	G.E.H. Beamish	IX-162
The Client-Consultant Questionnaire	W.W. Burke	'86-81
Communication Congruence Inventory (CCI)	M. Sashkin	'87-124

Training/Learning Style

Title	Author(s)	Volume & Page No.
Opinionnaire on Assumptions About Human Relations Training	J.E. Jones, J. Dickinson, & C. Dee	I-110
S-C (Student-Content) Teaching Inventory	M.S. Spier	'74-118
Training Style Inventory	R. Brostrom	'79-94
Learning-Style Inventory	R.T. Jacobs & B.S. Fuhrmann	'84-106
The Trainer Type Inventory (TTI)	M. Wheeler & J. Marshall	'86-93
The Learning-Model Instrument	K.L. Murrell	'87-115

GROUPS/TEAMS

Title	Author(s)	Volume & Page No.
Dependency-Intimacy Rating Form	J.E. Jones	I-84
Group-Climate Inventory		III-25
Group-Growth Evaluation Form		III-26
Postmeeting Reactions Form		III-30
Group-Behavior Questionnaire		III-39
Intentions and Choices Inventory		III-40
Team-Building: Sensing Interview Guide	J.E. Jones	III-76
Reactions to Group Situations Test	H.A. Thelen	'74-91
TORI Group Self-Diagnosis Scale	J.R. Gibb	'77-75
Phases of Integrated Problem Solving (PIPS)	W.C. Morris & M. Sashkin	'78-109
Meeting-Evaluation Scale	F. Burns & R.L. Gragg	'81-89
Work-Group Effectiveness Inventory	F. Burns & R.L. Gragg	'81-90
Learning-Group Process Scale	F. Burns & R.L. Gragg	'81-94
The Team Orientation and Behavior Inventory (TOBI)	L.D. Goodstein, P. Cooke, & J. Goodstein	'83-109
The Team Effectiveness Critique	M. Alexander	'85-105
Trust-Orientation Profile	M.R. Chartier	'91-135

INTERPERSONAL

Title	Author(s)	Volume & Page No.
Learning-Climate Analysis Form		III-36
Interpersonal Relationship Rating Scale	J.L. Hipple	'72-73
Johari Window Self-Rating Sheet	P.G. Hanson	'73-41
Scale of Feelings and Behavior of Love	C.H. Swensen & F. Gilner	'73-73
Self-Disclosure Questionnaire	S. M. Jourard	'74-104
Scale of Marriage Problems	C.H. Swensen & A.L. Fiore	'75-75
Problem-Analysis Questionnaire	B. Oshry & R. Harrison	'75-83
Organization Behavior Describer Survey (OBDS)	R. Harrison & B. Oshry	'76-105
Interpersonal Check List (ICL)	R. LaForge	'77-91
I Am, Don't You Think? Characteristics Sheet	J.C. Bryant	X-11
Self-Reliance Inventory	J.C. Quick, D.L. Nelson, & J.D. Quick	'91-149

MANAGEMENT/LEADERSHIP

General

Title	Author(s)	Volume & Page No.
Group Leadership Questionnaire (GTQ-C)	D.B. Wile	'72-91
Decision-Style Inventory	R. Roskin	'75-91
Leader Effectiveness and Adaptability Description (LEAD)	P. Hersey & K.H. Blanchard	'76-89
When to Delegate Inventory Sheet	T.F. Carney	VIII-55
Supervisory Behavior Questionnaire	H.P. Sims, Jr.	'81-98
Management Skills Inventory	C.J. Levin	IX-96
Styles Profile of Interaction Roles in Organizations (SPIRO)	U. Pareek	'84-126

Attitudes

Title	Author(s)	Volume & Page No.
T-P Leadership Questionnaire	*adapted from Sergiovanni, Metzcus, and Burden*	I-10
Supervisory Attitudes: The X-Y Scale	*adapted from R.N. Ford*	'72-67
LEAD (Leadership: Employee-Orientation and Differentiation) Questionnaire	R. Dore	'73-97
Increasing Employee Self-Control (IESC)	B.H. Harvey	'80-108
Managerial Attitude Questionnaire	R. Roskin	'82-110
Manager's Dilemma Work Sheet	R. Glaser & C. Glaser	'83-22
Sharing Perspectives Manager Sheet		X-130
The Supervisory and Leadership Beliefs Questionnaire	T.V. Rao	'86-118

ORGANIZATIONS

Diagnosis

Title	Author(s)	Volume & Page No.
Force-Field Analysis Inventory	*based on W.G. Bennis &* *S. Eisen*	II-82
OD Readiness Check List	J.W. Pfeiffer & J.E. Jones	'78-226
Power and OD Intervention Analysis (PODIA)	M. Sashkin and J.E. Jones	'79-102
Organizational Diagnosis Questionnaire	R.C. Preziosi	'80-115
Organizational-Process Survey	F. Burns & R.L. Gragg	'81-92
Conflict-Management Climate Index	B. Crosby & J.J. Scherer	'81-102
Communication Climate Inventory	J.I. Costigan & M.A. Schmeidler	'84-115
The Individual-Team-Organization (ITO) Survey	W. Anderson	'87-139
Organizational-Learning Diagnostics (OLD)	U. Pareek	'88-131
The Organizational-Health Survey	W. Phillips	'89-141
The HRD Climate Survey	T.V. Rao & E. Abraham	'90-143
Total Quality Management (TQM) Inventory	G. Reagan	'92-149

Employee Attitudes/Motivation

Title	Author(s)	Volume & Page No.
Motivation Feedback Opinionnaire	D.F. Michalak	'73-44
People on the Job Work Sheet	M.B. Ross	VIII-13
Quality of Work Life-Conditions/Feelings	M. Sashkin & J.J. Lengermann	'84-140
Sharing Perspectives Worker Sheet		X-131
Psychological Maturity Instrument (PMI)	W. Blank, J. Weitzel, G. Blau, & S.G. Green	'88-112
Motivational Analysis of Organizations-Climate (MAO-C)	U. Pareek	'89-161
Burnout Inventory	W.R. Warley	'92-121
Locus of Control Inventory	U. Pareek	'92-135

Values/Culture

Title	Author(s)	Volume & Page No.
Diagnosing Organization Ideology	R. Harrison	'75-103
Organizational Norms Opinionnaire	M. Alexander	'78-83
Sexual Values in Organizations Questionnaire	P. Morrison & R. DeGraw	VII-150
Management -Styles Spectrum	K.L. Murrell	'91-179

PERSONAL
General

Title	Author(s)	Volume & Page No.
Risk-Taking Behavior in Groups Questionnaire	R.R. Kurtz	IV-110
The Involvement Inventory	R. Heslin & B. Blake	'73-89
Inventory of Self-Actualizing Characteristics (ISAC)	A.G. Banet, Jr.	'76-70
Group Leader Self-Disclosure Scale	R.R. Dies	'77-70
Satisfaction Survey	A.J. Schuh	'79-88
Personal Style Inventory	R.C. Hogan & D.W. Champagne	'80-92
Life-Style Questionnaire	R. Driscoll & D.G. Eckstein	'82-102
Personality Traits Inventory	W.J. Schiller	IX-61
Work-Needs Assessment Inventory	P. Doyle	X-34
The Entrepreneurial Orientation Inventory	T.V. Rao	'85-135
Motivational Analysis of Organizations-Behavior (MAO-B)	U. Pareek	'86-121
Behavior Description	J.E. Oliver	'88-98
The Visibility/Credibility Inventory	W.B. Reddy & G. Williams	'88-119
The Cognitive-Style Inventory	L.P. Martin	'89-123
Inventory of Barriers to Creative Thought and Innovation Action	L.P. Martin	'90-131
Networking Skills Inventory	B. Byrum-Robinson & J.D. Womeldorff	'90-153
Inventory of Anger Communication (IAC)	M.J. Bienvenu, Sr.	'76-81

Conflict/Stress

Title	Author(s)	Volume & Page No.
Conflict-Management Style Survey	M. Robert	'82-83
Organizational Role Stress Scale	U. Pareek	'83-119
Role Pics	U. Pareek	'87-98
Life-Planning Program		II-103

Life Planning/Career Management

Title	Author(s)	Volume & Page No.
Role Efficacy Scale	U. Pareek	'80-103
Styles of Career Management	T. Carney	'83-96
The TEM Survey: An Assessment of Your Effectiveness in Managing Your Time, Energy, and Memory	G.J. Petrello	'83-126
Polarization: Opinionnaire on Womanhood	J.E. Jones & J.J. Jones	III-61

Values/Sexual Issues

Title	Author(s)	Volume & Page No.
Sex-Role Stereotyping Rating Scale	M. Carson	'73-28
Bem Sex-role Inventory (BSRI)	S.L. Bem	'77-86
Mach V Attitude Inventory	R. Christie	'78-99
Women as Managers Scale (WAMS)	J.R. Terborg	'79-82
The Personal Value Statement (PVS)	J.E. Oliver	'85-115
Attitudes Toward Women as Managers (ATWAM) Scale	E.B. Yost & T.T. Herbert	'85-123
Beyond-Personality Inventory: Archetypes of Change-Agent Style	J.J Coblentz	'90-115
Managerial Work-Values Scale	T.V. Rao	'91-163

INTRODUCTION TO LECTURETTES

Learning based on direct experience is not the only kind of learning appropriate to human-interaction training. Contrary to some criticisms of the field, group facilitators are not exclusively concerned with "gut-involved" experience; "head" learning is also valued.

The Role Of Cognitive Data

There has been, in the past, an "anti-head" bias among certain practitioners of human relations training. We believe, however, that the value of cognitive input in a training experience should not be discounted. Participants often would *rather* talk about their feelings, but some practical application of theory and research generally enriches laboratory training and may be essential in many types of cognitive and skill development. Feelings and "head" learning support, alter, validate, extend, and complement each other. Both affective and cognitive data are important in most types of training.

Lecture Method

Although the lecture method can easily be *overused*, it is one of the simplest ways of providing additional, vicarious learning for participants. Lecturettes are purposely simple and direct, with an emphasis on clarity and ease of presentation. They are not intended to be comprehensive or technical statements of theoretical positions. Each facilitator needs to develop a repertoire of theory and background that he or she can use in a variety of situations and activities.

One Of Four Major Components

However valid the use of the lecturette may be, it is only one of four major components utilized in designing training and development experiences.

The use of intensive small groups is the basic component of laboratory education. An almost endless variety of small groups exists.

Structured experiences of several types (for example, ice breakers, dyadic designs, or communication activities) help to generate and focus the data of a training event. The facilitator will find that a given structured experience can be equally appropriate in a personal-growth or leadership-development design, depending on the way the data are processed.

Measurement devices—instruments—are another component of a training workshop. They are useful in providing theory-based data with which participants can work in evaluating and understanding their learning experiences.

Advantages of the Lecturette

The lecturette, as the fourth major component included in a training design, can be used in several ways and for several purposes. It can be delivered in large-group sessions, commonly called "community" sessions. It can be used spontaneously in an intensive, small-group session. It can be offered to participants as an introduction to a group activity, as handout material during the activity, or in a summary session.

When a lecturette is provided by the facilitator as a "cognitive map" for the experience that is to follow, it can be a guide for the participants in transferring their learnings to their everyday experiences. As a method of focusing a participant's experiences in previous activities toward a theoretical model, it is highly effective. Thus the lecturette, when properly used, becomes a direct and useful means—for both participant and facilitator—of infusing cognitive material into the learning experience.

There is, of course, a potential pitfall in the use of lecturette material. We do not advocate "killing gnats with sledge hammers"; too much emphasis on cognitive material can reduce its effectiveness. The lecturette, like many other tools, requires a deft touch.

A GUIDE TO PRESENTING LECTURETTES

The facilitator who wants to present effective, well-received lecturettes may find some of the following points helpful.

Taking Risks

Before the presentation, the facilitator needs to understand and consider his or her own motivations, purposes for the lecturette, and audience. Risk taking is, however, a necessary element in presenting effective lecturettes; the facilitator should be prepared to juggle alternatives, change his or her mind, or offer unplanned asides; thus the facilitator models risk-taking behavior for the participants.

A Positive Approach

It is important to start the lecturette with a positive approach. The facilitator should establish contact with the participants and prepare them by telling them what he or she is going to do and why it will be interesting to them.

Useful Aids

The general considerations to be taken into account in the facilitator's actual discourse are useful aids, content, and manner of presentation. Uncomplicated visual aids such as charts and graphs are helpful; so are concrete, specific, personalized examples with which the audience can identify.

Effectiveness of Content

Whatever the subject matter, the facilitator can increase its acceptability by reminding the participants why it is important. The facilitator also can use humor (best if pointed toward himself or herself) to temper the intensity of the event, can strive to avoid jargon, and can offer a personal point of view about the material rather than simply report the ideas of others.

Presentation

How the facilitator presents the discourse is significant to its impact. Pacing the lecturette to accord with the audience is important. The facilitator should look for signs of puzzlement, incomprehension, or boredom and should slow down or speed up the presentation on the basis of these cues. Interrupting the discourse from time to time by initiating brief activities or by soliciting comments and examples from the audience also varies the pace of the presentation.

Voice modulation helps to keep the attention and interest of the audience; so does eye contact. The facilitator also should be aware of the physical setting and his or her own body language. Leftover posters tacked to the wall behind a speaker, for example, may present a continued, inappropriate distraction. Nervous or excessive gesturing may reduce the impact of what the facilitator is saying.

Except for direct quotations, the facilitator should not *read* the lecturette. Reading both reduces the personal touch and increases the audience's tendency to lose interest.

Since the presentation is oral, clarity is essential. A simple organization, a clearly delineated progression from point to point, appropriate restatements or recapitulations—these devices are simple but very helpful. It is often useful to visually present the outline of the lecturette.

Approach

Finally, the facilitator will be most effective if it is clear that he or she is excited about the subject, enthusiastic, natural and human, and having fun. The facilitator should neither be apologetic about the material or discount the value of what is being offered nor preach or berate opposing views.

After the presentation, the facilitator should summarize clearly, restating the significant points that were made; challenge the listeners to experiment with new behavior or new approaches; and encourage participants to take risks in applying new ideas.

Appropriately used and presented, the lecturette becomes an essential element—useful for both the facilitator and the participants—in the training experience.

CLASSIFICATION OF LECTURETTES

In the 1984 *Annual* and from that time on, lecturette materials that are directly related to or necessary for the use of a particular structured experience or instrument have been included within the text for that structured experience or instrument. This eliminates the need for the facilitator to search through various sections of the *Annual* in order to compile the materials for a complete presentation of a particular structured experience or instrument. *However,* some lecturette material of general interest and wide applicability still will be published from time to time and will appear in the new Professional Development section of the *Annual.* All lecturettes will continue to be categorized here in the *Reference Guide,* in order that facilitators looking for sources for brief, theoretical inputs will be able to locate such materials quickly and easily.

Each of the lecturettes classified in this *Reference Guide* is categorized according to its primary emphasis. As is the case in each of the sections of the Reference Guide to Handbooks and Annuals, this classification is somewhat arbitrary. Categories established for this section are the following:

Organizations
Personal Growth
Facilitation
Communication
Management/Leadership

ORGANIZATIONS

Title	Author(s)	Volume & Page No.
Job Enrichment	F.V. Jessey	'72-127
Management by Objectives	T.M. Thomson	'72-130
An Introduction to PERT...Or...	D.E. Yoes	'72-135
Kurt Lewin's "Force Field Analysis"	M.S. Spier	'73-111
Three Approaches to Organizational Learning	A.J. Reilly	'73-130
Personal and Organizational Pain: Costs and Profits	P.J. Runkel	'74-148
Participatory Management: A New Morality	J.A. Stepsis	'75-120
Skill Climate and Organizational Blockages	D.L. Francis	'75-126
Open Systems	D.J. Marion	'75-132
Handling Group and Organizational Conflict	D.T. Simpson	'77-120
Organizational Norms	M. Alexander	'77-123
The Organizational Gestalt	P. Scholtes	'78-149
The Emotional Cycle of Change	D. Kelley & D.R. Conner	'79-117
The Systems View of Organizations: Dynamics of Organizational Change	P.R. Luciano	'79-140
Team Building from a Gestalt Perspective	H.B. Karp	'80-157
Dealing with Organizational Crises	M. Sashkin & J.E. Jones	'80-166
Coping with Anarchy in Organizations	M.A. Berger	'81-135
Issues Present When Entering a System	R. Hensley	'82-140
Traditional Approaches to Consulting Versus a Collaborative Approach	J.J. Sherwood	'82-143
Checkpoints in the Contracting Process	L.D. Goodstein & D.M. Dawson	'82-147
An OD Flow Chart: From Beginning to End	W.R. Gamble	'82-150
A Look at Quality Circles	H.B. Karp	'83-157
Surviving Organizational Burnout	J.M. Shearer	'83-175
Measuring Excellence Theory Sheet	L.D. Goodstein	'85-84
The Team Effectiveness Critique	M. Alexander	'85-101
Work-Needs Assessment Theory Sheet	P. Doyle	X-39
Sticky Wickets Group-Stress Theory Sheet	W.B. Kline & J.J. Blase	X-103
Humanizing the Work Place	E. Schindler-Rainman	'87-197
Four Corners Theory Sheet	B. Jameson	'88-54
Humor and the Effective Work Group	J.M. Westcott	'88-139

ORGANIZATIONS (Continued)

Title	Author(s)	Volume & Page No.
The Robotics Decision Theory Sheet	C.H. Smith	'89-93
What's in It for Me? Theory Sheet	K. Kreis	'90-26
Bases of Power Information Sheet	M.H. Kitzmiller	'91-46
Multiple Roles Theory Sheet	M. Nandy	'91-92
Working at Our Company Theory Sheet	L.D. Goodstein	'92-84

PERSONAL GROWTH

Title	Author(s)	Volume & Page No.
Risk-Taking and Error Protection Styles	J.E. Jones	'72-113
Defense Mechanisms in Groups	P. Thoresen	'72-117
Assumptions About the Nature of Man	J.E. Jones	'72-119
The Maslow Need Hierarchy	S.L. Pfeiffer	'72-125
The Johari Window: A Model for Soliciting and Giving Feedback	P.G. Hanson	'73-114
Risk-Taking	J.W. Pfeiffer	'73-124
Dependency and Intimacy	J.E. Jones	'73-132
Thinking and Feeling	A.G. Banet, Jr.	'73-139
Figure/Ground	J.A. Pfeiffer	'74-131
Humanistic Numbers	J.E. Jones	'75-115
Human Needs and Behavior	A.J. Reilly	'75-123
Re-Entry	J.E. Jones	'75-129
Assertion Theory	C. Kelley	'76-115
Interpersonal Feedback as Consensual Validation of Constructs	D.A. Devine	'76-124
Making Judgments Descriptive	A.C. Filley & L.A. Pace	'76-128
Power	D.C. King & J.C. Glidewell	'76-139
Centering	A.G. Banet, Jr.	'77-99
Androgyny	J. Campbell	'77-102
The Pendulum Swing: A Necessary Evil in the Growth Cycle	B.A. Gaw	'78-143
How to Maintain Personal Energy	J.E. Jones	'79-113
Jealousy: A Proactive Approach	C. Kelley	'80-138

PERSONAL GROWTH (Continued)

Title	Author(s)	Volume & Page No.
Job-Related Adaptive Skills: Toward Personal Growth	J.J. Scherer	'80-152
Thinking About Feelings	W.C. Boshear	'81-117
Stress-Management Skills: Self-Modification for Personal Adjustment to Stress	L.P.K. LeGras	'81-138
Intrapersonal Conflict Resolution	H. Pates	'81-141
Three Forces in Psychology	M. Sashkin	'82-132
Coping with Conflict	M.B. Ross	'82-135
Preventing and Resolving Conflict	U. Pareek	'83-164
Gaining Support Theory Sheet	J. Spoth, B.H. Morris, & T.C. Denton	'85-42
Creating Ideal Personal Futures: The Nature of Personal Premises	J.D. Adams	'88-35
Control or Surrender Theory Sheet	J. Ballard	'89-51

FACILITATION

Title	Author(s)	Volume & Page No.
Guidelines for Group Member Behavior	J.W. Pfeiffer	'72-109
A Model of Group Development	J.E. Jones	'73-127
Cog's Ladder: A Model of Group Development	G.O. Charrier	'74-142
Common Problems in Volunteer Groups	E. Bancroft	'75-111
Wishes and Fears	A. G. Banet, Jr.	'75-118
Training Components for Group Facilitators	R.K. Conyne	'75-138
Therapy or Personal Growth?	T.A. Boone	'75-141
Alternatives to Theorizing	S.M. Herman	'76-143
Strategies for Designing an Intervention	G.H. Varney	'78-133
Contracting: A Process and a Tool	F. L. Ulschak	'78-138
Stages of Group Development	P.P. Fay & A.G. Doyle	'82-124
Major Growth Processes in Groups	J.E. Jones	'82-128
Using Humor in Workshops	J. Goodman	'83-137
The Seven Pieces Lecturette on Group Roles	N.J. Carpenter	'84-20

FACILITATION (Continued)

Title	Author(s)	Volume & Page No.
Up Close and Personal with Dr. Maslow Theory Sheet	B. Jameson	'92-115
Up Close and Personal with Dr. Maslow Resource Sheet	B. Jameson	'92-117
Group Size as a Function of Trust	P. Leone	'92-185

COMMUNICATION

Title	Author(s)	Volume & Page No.
Synergy and Consensus-Seeking	J.E. Jones	'73-108
Conditions Which Hinder Effective Communication	J.W. Pfeiffer	'73-120
Confrontation: Types, Conditions, and Outcomes	R.R. Kurtz & J.E. Jones	'73-135
Five Components Contributing to Effective Interpersonal Communications	M.R. Chartier	'74-125
Making Requests Through Metacommunication	C.M. Rossiter, Jr.	'74-129
The Interpersonal Contract	C.G. Carney & S.L. McMahon	'74-135
Communication Patterns in Organization Structure	D.L. Ford, Jr. & O. Elliott	'74-150
Dealing with Anger	J.E. Jones & A.G. Banet, Jr.	'76-111
The Awareness Wheel	S. Miller, F.W. Nunnally, & D.B. Wackman	'76-120
D-I-D: A Three-Dimensional Model for Understanding Group Communication	D.G. Smith	'77-106
Constructive Conflict in Discussions: Learning to Manage Disagreements Effectively	J.T. Wood	'77-115
Communication Effectiveness: Active Listening and Sending Feeling Messages	J.N. Wismer	'78-119
Communicating Communication	J.R. Luthi	'78-123
Anybody with Eyes Can See the Facts!	A. Kuperman	'79-128
The Four-Communication-Styles Approach	T. Carney	'80-127
Interaction Process Analysis	B. Byrum-Gaw	'80-133
Defensive and Supportive Communication	G.W. Combs	'81-113
Kenepathy	M. Stimac	'81-124

COMMUNICATION (Continued)

Title	Author(s)	Volume & Page No.
Stress, Communication, and Assertiveness: A Framework for Interpersonal Problem Solving	B.D. Ruben	'83-170
Taking Responsibility Theory Sheet	G.L. Talbot	X-65
Poor Listening Habits Theory Sheet	J. Seltzer & L.W. Howe	'87-29
Poor Listening Habits: Effective Listening Sheet	J. Seltzer & L.W. Howe	'87-30
E-Prime Theory Sheet	H.B. Karp	'88-143
A Positive Approach to Resistance	H.B. Karp	'88-143
The Art of Feedback Principles	S.C. Bushardt & A.R. Fowler, Jr.	'89-13
What's Legal? Clarification Sheet	R.J. Cantwell	'89-34
Quality Customer Service Idea Sheet	B. Jameson	'91-32
The Parking Space Theory Sheet	F.E. Jandt	'91-39
Conflict Management Suggestion Sheet	L.C. Porter	'91-122
Feedback Awareness Theory Sheet	R.W. Lucas	'92-33

MANAGEMENT/LEADERSHIP

Title	Author(s)	Volume & Page No.
McGregor's Theory X-Theory Y Model	A.J. Robinson	'72-121
Criteria of Effective Goal-Setting: The SPIRO Model	J.E. Jones	'72-133
Win/Lose Situations	G.E. Wiley	'73-105
Hidden Agendas		'74-133
Conflict-Resolution Strategies	J.A. Stepsis	'74-139
The "Shouldist" Manager	S.M. Herman	'74-146
The Supervisor as Counselor	R.A. Zawacki & P.E. LaSota	'75-135
Leadership as Persuasion and Adaptation	J.T. Wood	'76-132
Role Functions in a Group	D. Nylen, J.R. Mitchell, & A. Stout	'76-136
A Practical Leadership Paradigm	T.A. Boone	'77-110
Tolerance of Equivocality: The Bronco, Easy Rider, Blockbuster, and Nomad	R.C. Rodgers	'78-128
Encouraging Others To Change Their Behavior	J.C. Morton & D.M. Blair	'79-123

MANAGEMENT/LEADERSHIP (Continued)

Title	Author(s)	Volume & Page No.
The Centered Boss	P. Scholtes	'79-133
Transactions in the Change Process	T.R. Harvey	'79-136
Dimensions of Role Efficacy	U. Pareek	'80-143
A Nine-Step Problem-Solving Model	L.C. Earley & P. B. Rutledge	'80-146
Dealing with Disruptive Individuals in Meetings	J.E. Jones	'80-161
Creativity and Creative Problem Solving	M.B. Ross	'81-129
A Structured Format for Improving Meetings	J.J. Rosenblum	'82-121
Encouragement: Giving Positive Invitations	D.G. Eckstein	'83-142
Toward More Effective Meetings	M.M. Milstein	'83-145
A Guide to Problem Solving	D. Elias & P. David	'83-149
Management Perspectives Theory Sheet	P. Doyle	'85-53
Raises Theory Sheet	A.J. Schuh	'86-69
The Lost Art of Feedback	H. Karp	'87-237
Delegation Theory Sheet	M.M. O'Malley & C.M.T. Lombardozzi	'88-84
Four Factors Theory Sheet	W.N. Parker	'89-42
Words Apart Theory Sheet	M. Maier	'90-32
Rhetoric and Behavior Theory Sheet	M. Vanterpool	'91-55

INTRODUCTION TO PROFESSIONAL DEVELOPMENT (FORMERLY "THEORY AND PRACTICE") PAPERS

In human resource development, in leadership and management development, in organization development, in the consulting process, in the whole training field, we believe that the most critical component is the personal, *human* element. Theory, technique, and research are important and invaluable, but they should be seen in perspective, against a framework of the human, the personal, the individual, the practical, and the *real*.

DIMENSIONS OF FACILITATOR EFFECTIVENESS

The Person
Empathy
Acceptance
Congruence
Flexibility

Skills
Listening
Expressing Oneself
Observing
Responding
Intervening
Designing

Techniques
Structured Experiences
Instruments
Lecturettes
Confrontations
Interventions (Verbal and Nonverbal)

Theories
Personality
Group Dynamics
Organizational Behavior
Systems
Community Behavior

The Person

Social ills continue to plague us despite our current, incredible technology. We need to learn more about our own interpersonal relationships—and this is what the field of human resource development and training is about. The common denominator is the *person*. To become better as a facilitator, one must become better as a person.

One of the significant personal dimensions is the ability to *feel empathy* for another person. Complete empathy is not possible, of course; we can never fully experience someone else's situation. But we can try to see things from another person's perspective; this effort is critical.

Acceptance is another important personal dimension—allowing another person to be different, to have a different set of values and goals, to behave differently. Rogers calls this unconditional positive regard (UPR).

Congruence and *flexibility* are two additional aspects of the person. A congruent person is aware of what he or she is doing and feeling and is able to communicate that self to another person in a straightforward way. A healthy and psychologically mature person is flexible, not dogmatic, opinionated, rigid, or authoritarian. A healthy consultant should be able to deal with another person at that person's pace.

If people have these personal attributes, they are therapeutic. Just being around them makes others feel good; they help by being well-integrated persons themselves.

The most meaningful direction consultants can take is toward improving their own personal development, furthering their own understanding of their values, attitudes, impulses, and desires. Two major interpersonal conflicts that facilitators must be able to resolve for themselves are their individual capacities for intimacy and their relations to authority.

Important as the personal dimension is, however, there are other components involved in successful human resource development and other areas of training and consulting.

Skills

Certain basic communicating skills are necessary in order to promote individual, group, and organizational growth. A facilitator needs to develop the ability to *listen,* to *express* (both verbally and nonverbally), to *observe,* to *respond* to people, to *intervene* artfully in the group process, and to *design* effective learning environments that make efficient use of resources.

Techniques

One also can heighten and improve the effect of training and consulting through certain techniques. Structured experiences, instruments, lecturettes, confrontations, and verbal and nonverbal interventions are all useful in increasing a facilitator's effectiveness.

Theories

Theory is a resource. It is one of the components a facilitator uses to develop and improve as a practitioner.

Theories abound in applied behavioral science; there are theories of personality, group dynamics, organizational behavior, community behavior, and systems.

Systems theory, for example, has some interesting implications for OD in that it points out that all systems are interdependent and that no one can be dealt with in isolation.

Practice

At the moment, many training and development practitioners are far ahead of theorists: the tendency is to try out an idea and see if it works first and then to find the research underpinnings necessary for its justification. Explanation follows practice.

Theory and research are inextricably intertwined with practice—one requires the other. Yet if the choice had to be made between a brilliant theorist, thoroughly grounded in technique and theory, and a stimulating, effective consultant with a well-integrated personal self, many practitioners would choose the latter.

PERSPECTIVE ON TRAINING AND CONSULTING

Historically, four streams of work have characterized the field of human interaction training: personal growth, leadership and management development, organization development, and community development. The major element that exists across these spheres of interest is the use of intensive small groups as interventions in training activities. While the use of the small group remains, the spheres themselves seem to be less distinct, blending into an approach that takes into account the people within the organization—as well as their subgroupings—to result in a more unified approach to the system as a whole. This new consciousness includes aspects of long-range strategic planning, organization development, community and team-building efforts, and development of individuals within the system—some of what used to be called "personnel" functions. The term that seems to be used most often to describe this approach is human resource development (HRD). In short, more effort is being paid to seeing that the individuals within the organization are heading in the same direction as the organization, and preferably at the same pace.

From its conception, human resource development seemed to lie primarily within the scope of organization development professionals—trainers and consultants. The chart that follows illustrates some of the overlap among the four historical areas of training and development activity.

The four columns of the chart are cumulative to the right; that is, the *individual* is the basic ingredient of the *group,* which is the basic building block of *organizations,* which make up the basis of *communities.* Within each of these four classifications there is an *intra* and *inter* dimension. The *intra-individual* cell of the chart represents the locus of personal growth activities. We are concerned in personal growth with helping individual participants grow in awareness of their

The Four Major Areas of Activity in Training

	Individual	Group	Organization	Community

I N T R A	**Personal Growth**
	sensory awareness
	value clarification
	life planning
		Leadership Development
		Organization Development
		group dynamics
		team building
			Organization Development
			planning
			systems
			climate
			  assessment
			managing
			  change
			problem solving
			managing
			  conflict
			
			Human Resource Development
			manpower
			  planning
			skills
			  development
			performance
			  appraisal
			management
			  development
				Community Development

I N T E R	**Personal Growth**
	Professional (Task) Growth
	Leadership Development
	communication
	  skills
	human interaction
	management
	  development
		Leadership Development
		Organization Development
		negotiation
		  skills
		group
		  dynamics
			Organization Development
			Community Development
			mergers	

feelings, attitudes, values, and self-concepts, and these traits are presumed to be primarily intrapsychic.

In the *interindividual* cell of the chart we see that personal-growth activities and leadership-development activities overlap in their emphasis on human inter-action. Both leadership and management development, on the one hand, and personal growth activities, on the other, share a common concern with building skills for effective human interactions, such as listening, expressing oneself, and responding to others.

In the *intragroup* cell of the chart, we can see that facilitators have as a common basis an emphasis on understanding and intervening in group dynamics. In-tragroup phenomena such as participation, influence, decision making, and task versus process orientation become the basis for many interventions in personal growth, leadership development, and organization development. Organizations are primarily made up of individual people who are members of overlapping, embedded groups, and the consultant needs to be sensitive to the fact that the dynamics within the groups can materially affect the problem-solving capability of the organization. Team building has a great deal in common with both leadership development and personal-growth training. It is little wonder, then, that group facilitators most often enter organization development at the level of team building.

Leadership-development and organization-development workers share a common interest in studying *intergroup* phenomena. Such aspects of organiza-tional life as cooperation and competition across groups and sharing of informa-tion become a concern both in training leaders and in working real organizational issues.

The core of organization development is in the *intraorganization* cell of the chart. The OD consultant is concerned with monitoring and intervening in such systemic processes as influence, communication patterns, morale, and utilization of human resources. The effort is to look at the total organization as composed of interdependent subsystems.

It is in the *interorganization* sphere that OD specialists and community-devel-opment workers share a common interest. Communities can be seen as consisting of relatively autonomous but interdependent organizations. These may be schools, churches, social-service agencies, manufacturing organizations, or busi-nesses, which may or may not recognize their dependency on one another. The OD consultant is concerned with seeing how the organization "interfaces" with its environment, including its customers and suppliers as well as pressure groups in the environment, such as the government and political organizations. The com-munity-development consultant is concerned with how the organizations in a given community interrelate in ways that affect the "common good."

There are basically two types of community-development change agents. The activists, trained in political power interventions and characterized by Saul Alinsky and Cesar Chavez, advocate particular types of community reform through the use of collective strategies for garnering power. The consultant who is oriented toward applied behavioral science, however, operates primarily from a confrontive stance, attempting to get organizations in the community to look at the processes through which they relate to one another, in order to increase their ability to collaborate. This job is the most complex in the four types of training activities, in that the consultant has to deal with highly mixed motives and often must rely on volunteers to carry out decisions spawned by the processes he or she has sponsored.

The complexity in training and development work has increased with its emergent technology. The emphasis on personal development has been traditional almost from the beginning of the development of this field. Organization development has less history than management development, and community development as an applied behavioral science field is quite new in comparison. The place to be occupied by human resource development in this complex tapestry is still being defined. What is clear, however, is that each area of specialty has much to learn from, and much to contribute to, the others.

CLASSIFICATION OF PROFESSIONAL DEVELOPMENT (FORMERLY "THEORY AND PRACTICE") PAPERS

In the 1984 *Annual,* we introduced the "Professional Development" section, which includes the type of contents previously found in the Lecturettes, Theory and Practice, and Resources sections of the 1972-1983 *Annuals.* This allows us more flexibility in integrating information—expository text with a bibliography, for example—and more accurately describes the purpose of the articles, listings, and other materials that will appear in this section.

For ease and clarity in finding materials in this *Reference Guide,* lecturettes (whether they are found in structured experiences, in the introductions to instruments, or as separate pieces in the Professional Development section) will continue to be classified in the "Lecturettes" section of this book. Similarly, bibliographies, book reviews, and listings of product sources or professional affiliations will continue to be classified in the "Resources" section of this *Reference Guide.* Articles that present new ideas or perspectives, new techniques or developments, and discussions of specific content areas will be classified in this section, as before.

The papers published in the Theory and Practice sections of the 1972-1983 *Annuals* and the Professional Development sections of the 1984-1992 *Annuals* fall into six categories:

> Organization Development
> Design
> Communication
> Models
> Facilitation
> Research

We have not attempted to maintain a balanced distribution of articles in these categories in the papers we publish. The *Annual* serves a function quite different from scholarly journals; its materials are written and edited to be immediately useful to the practitioner.

ORGANIZATION DEVELOPMENT

Title	Author(s)	Volume & Page No.
An Introduction to Organization Development	J.J. Sherwood	'72-153
Seven Pure Strategies of Change	K.E. Olmosk	'72-163
Notes on Freedom	S.M. Herman	'72-211
Planned Renegotiation: A Norm-Setting OD Intervention	J.J. Sherwood & J.C. Glidewell	'73-195
Some Implications of Value Clarification for Organization Development	M. Smith	'73-203
The Sensing Interview	J.E. Jones	'73-213
An Informal Glossary of Terms and Phrases in Organization Development	P.B. Vaill	'73-235
Individual Needs and Organizational Goals: An Experiential Lecture	A.J. Reilly	'74-215
Basic Concepts of Survey Feedback	D.G. Bowers & J.L. Franklin	'74-221
Team-Building	A.J. Reilly & J.E. Jones	'74-227
The Shadow of Organization Development	S.M. Herman	'74-239
Managing the Dynamics of Change and Stability	A. Broskowski, W.L. Mermis, Jr., & F. Khajavi	'75-173
The White Paper: A Tool for OD	T.H. Patten, Jr.	'75-195
Understanding Your Organization's Character	R. Harrison	'75-199
A Gestalt Approach to Collaboration in Organizations	H.B. Karp	'76-203
A Current Assessment of OD: What It Is and Why It Often Fails	J.W. Pfeiffer & J.E. Jones	'76-225
Team Development: A Training Approach	L.N. Solomon	'77-181
Intervening in Organizations Through Reward Systems	T.H. Patten, Jr.	'77-195
Constructive Citizen Participation	D.M. Connor	'77-209
Utilizing Human Resources: Individual Versus Group Approaches to Problem Solving and Decision Making	J.J. Sherwood & F.J. Hoylman	'78-157
Types of Process Interventions	A.M. Freedman	'78-163
OD Readiness	J.W. Pfeiffer & J.E. Jones	'78-219
The Behavioral Science Roots of Organization Development: An Integrated Perspective	T.H. Patten, Jr.	'79-194

ORGANIZATION DEVELOPMENT (Continued)

Title	Author(s)	Volume & Page No.
Alternative Data-Feedback Designs for Organizational Intervention	D.A. Nadler	'79-221
Consultation to Human-Service Programs	L.D. Goodstein	'80-213
Evaluation of Human-Service Programs	K.S. Trisko & V.C. League	'80-224
Multiple Measures to Assess the Impact of Organization Development Interventions	D.L. Lockwood & F. Luthans	'80-233
Developing Collaboration in Organizations	U. Pareek	'81-165
Human Resource Development: What It Is and How To Become Involved	J.E. Jones	'81-188
An Overview of Ten Management and Organizational Theorists	M. Sashkin	'81-206
A Method for Structured Naturalistic Observation of Organizational Behavior	D.N.T. Perkins, D.A. Nadler, & M.D. Hanlon	'81-222
Holistic Human Resource Development: Beyond Techniques and Procedures	R. Kaufman	'82-208
Organizational Health in Small Enterprises	R.R. Bates	'83-181
Managing Supervisory Transition	R.J. Zugel	'83-231
Organizational Analysis, Design, and Implementation: An Approach for Improving Effectiveness	D.A. Nadler	'83-241
Human Resource Development: Current Status and Future Directions	L.D. Goodstein & J.W. Pfeiffer	'84-155
OD with a Management Perspective	J.C. Lewis	'84-168
Organizational Use of the Behavioral Sciences: The Improbable Task	W. Bennis	'84-176
Organization Development and Power	W.F.G. Mastenbroek	'84-188
An Organization Development (OD) Primer	L.D. Goodstein & P. Cooke	'84-207
A Guide to Participative Management	M. Sashkin	'84-227
The Expectancy Theory of Motivation: Implications for Training and Development	J.A. Sample	'84-257
Encouraging Managers To Deal with Marginal Employees	J.W. Pfeiffer	'84-282
A Taxonomy of Intergroup Conflict-Resolution Strategies	D.C. Feldman	'85-169
Functional Roles for Facilitating Organizational Change	M.R. Chartier	'85-177

ORGANIZATION DEVELOPMENT (Continued)

Title	Author(s)	Volume & Page No.
Considerations for Managers in Implementing Change	P. Doyle	'85-183
Institutionalization of Planned Organizational Change: A Model and Review of the Literature	P.F. Buller, B.O. Saxberg, & H.L. Smith	'85-189
A Situational Leadership Approach to Groups Using the Tuckman Model of Group Development	C. Kormanski	'85-217
Creating Conditions that Encourage Mentoring	K.E. Kram	'85-239
Managing the Arational in Organizations and Institutions	G. Egan	'85-259
Applied Strategic Planning: A New Model for Organizational Growth and Vitality	L.D. Goodstein, J.W. Pfeiffer, & T.M. Nolan	'85-275
The HRD Professional: Master of Many Roles	T.W. Goad	'86-137
Similarities and Differences Between Internal and External Consulting	L.D. McDermott	'86-145
Human Resource Development in a Changing World	G.L. Lippitt	'86-177
Developing and Increasing Role Efficacy	U. Pareek	'86-201
Cultural Synergy: Managing the Impact of Cultural Diversity	N.J. Adler	'86-229
Structuring the OD Function in Corporate America	B.B. Bunker	'86-239
Competence in Managing Lateral Relations	W.W. Burke & C.A. Coruzzi	'87-151
Impact at Ground Zero: Where Theory Meets Practice	P. Doyle & C.R. Tindal	'87-157
Toward Functional Organizational Development: What to Do After the Search and the Passion for Excellence	R. Kaufman	'87-169
Why Employee Involvement Often Fails and What It Takes to Succeed	B. Crosby	'87-179
Forecasting the Economic Benefits of Training	R.A. Swanson & G.D. Geroy	'87-213
Organizations and the Search for Approval	A. Johnson	'88-163
Organization Development: The Evolution to "Excellence" and Corporate Culture	T.H. Patten, Jr.	'88-189
Quality Circles: After the Honeymoon	E.E. Lawler III & S.A. Mohrman	'88-201
Outstanding Performance Through Superteams	J. Pokora & W. Briner	'88-215

ORGANIZATION DEVELOPMENT (Continued)

Title	Author(s)	Volume & Page No.
The Conference as Context for Implementing Organizational-Improvement Strategies	L.D. Terry	'88-223
Task Analysis for Human Resource Development	U. Pareek	'88-245
Strategies for Helping Managers to Downsize Organizations	L.C. McDermott	'88-255
Creative Risk Taking	R.E. Byrd & J.L. Byrd	'89-211
Leadership Is in the Eye of the Follower	J.M. Kouzes & B.Z. Posner	'89-233
Fostering Intrapreneurship in Organizations	G. Pinchot III	'89-241
A Model for the Executive Management of Transformational Change	R. Beckhard	'89-255
Needs Assessment: Forerunner to Successful HRD Programs	A. Rossett	'90-191
Characteristics of Successful Organization Development: A Review of the Literature	P.G. Walters	90-209
Sexual Harassment of Women in the Workplace: Managerial Strategies for Understanding, Preventing, and Limiting Liability	J.L. Carbonell, J. Higginbotham, & J. Sample	'90-225
Linking Strategic Planning to the Management of People	M.C. Busch	'90-265
Central Issues in Career Planning	D.C. Feldman	'90-271
Legendary Customer Service and the HRD Professional's Role	G.M. Heil & R.W. Tate	'90-281
Evaluation and Management Development	N.M. Dixon	'91-287
The Manager as Leader in an Empowering Organization: Opportunities and Challenges	K.L. Murrell & J.F. Vogt	'91-297
Developing Successful Job Aids	A. Rossett & J. Gautier-Downes	'91-189
Career Planning and the Fallacy of the Future	P. Doyle & J. Zabel	'92-207
From Controlling to Facilitating: How to L.E.A.D.	F. Rees	'92-213
Managing Diversity in the Workplace	S.K. Kogod	'92-241
Using Personality Typology to Build Understanding	T. La Motta	'92-263
Managing Green: Defining an Organization's Environmental Role	M.K. Prokop	'92-275

DESIGN (relates to training design)

Title	Author(s)	Volume & Page No.
Contracts in Encounter Groups	G. Egan	'72-185
The Concept of Structure in Experiential Learning	R.R. Middleman & G. Goldberg	'72-203
Counseling and Clinical Training Applications of Human Relations Theory and Practice	R. Levin	'72-225
Design Considerations in Laboratory Education	J.W. Pfeiffer & J.E. Jones	'73-177
A Two-Phase Approach to Human Relations Training	G. Egan	'73-225
Life/Work Planning	A.G. Kirn & M. Kirn	'74-189
Cybernetic Sessions: A Technique for Gathering Ideas	J.T. Hall & R.A. Dixon	'74-197
The Experiential Learning Model and Its Application to Large Groups	S.E. Marks & W.L. Davis	'75-161
Applied Group Problem-Solving: The Nominal Group Technique	D.L. Ford, Jr., & P.M. Nemiroff	'75-179
Designing and Facilitating Experiential Group Activities: Variables and Issues	C.L. Cooper & K. Harrison	'76-157
The Delphi Technique: A Projection Tool for Serious Inquiry	R.L. Bunning	'79-174
Meeting Management	D. Nicoll	'81-183
An Introduction to Life-Style Assessment	D.G. Eckstein & R. Driscoll	'82-182
Modeling: Teaching by Living the Theory	B. Byrum-Gaw & C. J. Carlock	'83-187
Dance/Movement Therapy: A Primer for Group Facilitators	S.F. Wallock & D.G. Eckstein	'83-195
Video-Enhanced Human Relations Training: Self-Modeling and Behavior Rehearsal in Groups	J.L. Fryrear & S.A. Schneider	'83-203
A Model for Training Design: Selecting Appropriate Methods	D.T. Simpson	'83-223
Needs Assessment: Avoiding the "Hammer" Approach	J. Thomas	'84-195
Developing a Training System	R.P. Lynton & U. Pareek	'86-171
Diagnosing the Training Situation: Matching Instructional Techniques with Learning Outcomes and Environment	C.R. Kay, S.K. Peyton, & R. Pike	'87-203
The Nuts and Bolts of Assertiveness Training	B. Byrum	'88-147
Designing More Effective Orientation Programs	D.C. Feldman	'88-179

DESIGN (relates to training design) (Continued)

Title	Author(s)	Volume & Page No.
New Age Training Technologies: The Best and the Safest	B. Byrum	'89-183
Evaluation: Issues First, Methodology Second	P. Cooke & R.R. Bates	'89-223

COMMUNICATION

Title	Author(s)	Volume & Page No.
Communication Modes: An Experiential Lecture	J.E. Jones	'72-173
Openness, Collusion and Feedback	J.W. Pfeiffer & J.E. Jones	'72-197
"Don't You Think That....?": An Experiential Lecture on Indirect and Direct Communication	J.W. Pfeiffer & J.E. Jones	'74-203
Giving Feedback: An Interpersonal Skill	P.G. Hanson	'75-147
Nonverbal Communication and the Intercultural Encounter	M. Schnapper	'75-155
Clarity of Expression in Interpersonal Communication	M.R. Chartier	'76-149
Jargon: Rediscovering a Powerful Tool	L. Ren	'82-159
Understanding and Improving Communication Effectiveness	G.J. Rath & K.S. Stoyanoff	'82-166
The Art of Creative Fighting	H.B. Karp	'83-214
Interpersonal Feedback: Problems and Reconceptualization	R.V. Rasmussen	'84-262
Use of the Collaborative Ethic and Contingency Theories in Conflict Management	S.H. Taft	'87-187
The Feelings Vocabulary: A Tool for HRD Professionals	K.L. Dovey & W.L. Summer	'90-185
Negotiation Today: Everyone Wins	B. Byrum-Robinson	'91-199
Face-to-Face Selling for Consultants	D.M. Schrello	'91-225

MODELS

Title	Author(s)	Volume & Page No.
Types of Growth Groups	J.E. Jones	'72-145
TORI Theory and Practice	J.R. Gibb	'72-157

MODELS (Continued)

Title	Author(s)	Volume & Page No.
Transcendence Theory	J.W. Pfeiffer	'72-179
A Transactional Analysis Primer	J.P. Anderson	'73-145
Hill Interaction Matrix (HIM) Conceptual Framework for Understanding Groups	W.F. Hill	'73-159
Models and Roles of Change Agents	M. Sashkin	'74-209
A Gestalt Primer	J.W. Pfeiffer & J.A. Pfeiffer	'75-183
Dimensions of the Organizational Universe: A Model for Assessment and Direction	D.J. Marion	'75-211
Yin\Yang: A Perspective on Theories of Group Development	A.G. Banet, Jr.	'76-169
Interrole Exploration	U. Pareek	'76-211
A Tavistock Primer	A.G. Banet, Jr., & C. Hayden	'77-155
Structure as an Integrative Concept in Management Theory and Practice	J.A. Stepsis	'77-169
Personal Effectiveness	U. Pareek	'78-170
Loevinger's Ego States as the Basis of an Intervention Model	V. Pinedo, Jr.	'78-192
Behavioral Clarity in Consultation: The Triadic Model as Instrument	G. Egan	'78-204
Finishing Unfinished Business: Creative Problem Solving	F.L. Ulschak	'79-154
A Practical Model of Motivation and Character Development	R. Harrison	'79-207
Methods of Centering	A.G. Banet, Jr.	'80-175
Learning Cycles: Models of Behavioral Change	A.B. Palmer	'81-147
The Organizational Universe	J.E. Jones	'81-155
An Adlerian Primer	D.G. Eckstein	'81-193
Internal and External Control	U. Pareek	'82-174
Group Process Demystified	R.L. Burton	'82-190
Line Managers and Human Resource Development	U. Pareek & T.V. Rao	'84-161
Sociotechnical Systems Thinking in Management Consulting: A Holistic Concept for Organization Development	A. Zobrist & R.E. Enggist	'84-216
The Transformational Manager: Facilitating the Flow State	L.S. Ackerman	'84-242

MODELS (Continued)

Title	Author(s)	Volume & Page No.
The Support Model	J. Spoth, B.H. Morris, & T.C. Denton	'85-141
A Creative Problem-Solving Technique	J.E. Latting	'85-163
Integrated Human Resource Development Systems	T.V. Rao	'85-227
Power to the Practitioner	H.B. Karp	'86-151
Constructive Negotiation	W.F.G. Mastenbroek	'86-157
Delegation: A Process As Well As a Strategy	A. Lowy & P. Finestone	'86-163
STRIDE: The Breakthrough Process	J. Scherer	'86-185
The Use of Behaviorally Based Scales in Performance Appraisal	J.A. Sample	'86-191
A Primer on Social Styles	B. Byrum	'86-213
Career Stages and Life Stages: A Career-Development Perspective	D.C. Feldman	'87-225
A New Model of Team Building: A Technology for Today and Tomorrow	C. Kormanski & A. Mozenter	'87-255
A Model for Innovation	T.M. Nolan & S.J. Nolan	'88-171
Applying a Consulting Model to Managerial Behavior	T. Newell	'88-229
Model A: A Design Assessment and Facilitation Template in the Pursuit of Excellence	G. Egan	'89-267
A Causal Model of Organizational Performance	W.W. Burke & G.H. Litwin	'89-277
Overcoming Mind Traps: Self-Change and Its Implications for the HRD Professional	T. Rusk	'90-171
Performance Coaching	U. Pareek & T.V. Rao	'90-249
Codependence: Learned Dysfunctional Behavior	J.A. Pfeiffer	'91-215
A Matrix for Evaluating Training	J. Goodstein & L.D. Goodstein	'91-267
Emotional Isolation and Loneliness: Executive Problems	J.C. Quick, D.L. Nelson, J.R. Joplin, & J.D. Quick	'92-165
Time-Based Evolution and Faster Cycle Time	K.W. Herzog	'92-251

FACILITATION

Title	Author(s)	Volume & Page No.
Therapeutic Intervention and the Perception of Process	A.G. Banet, Jr.	'74-179
Co-Facilitating	J.W. Pfeiffer & J.E. Jones	'75-219
Working with Couples: Some Basic Considerations	H.A. Otto	'76-185
Fantasy: Theory and Technique	A.G. Banet, Jr., & J.E. Jones	'76-191
Consulting Process in Action	R. Lippitt & G.L. Lippitt	'77-129
Consultant Burnout	M.D. Mitchell	'77-143
Toward Androgynous Trainers	M. Sprague & A. Sargent	'77-147
Ethical Considerations in Consulting	J.W. Pfeiffer & J.E. Jones	'77-217
Configurational Learning: Principles for Facilitating Change and Learning from Experience	S. Farry	'78-179
Processing Questions: An Aid to Completing the Learning Cycle	B.A. Gaw	'79-147
Role Playing	J.E. Jones & J.W. Pfeiffer	'79-182
Accelerating the Stages of Group Development	J.J. Scherer	'80-182
Organizing and Conducting Microlabs for Training	T.V. Rao & U. Pareek	'80-191
Videotape Techniques for Small Training Groups	J.L. Fryrear	'80-199
A Strategy for Managing "Cultural" Transitions: Re-Entry from Training	A. Freedman	'80-204
Group Energy, Group Stage, and Leader Interventions	C.J. Carlock & B. Byrum-Gaw	'82-198
The Use of the Training Contract	H.B. Karp	'85-147
Videotapes and Vicarious Learning: A Technology for Effective Training	D.A. Gioia & H.P. Sims, Jr.	'85-155
Diagnosing and Changing Group Norms	D.C. Feldman	'85-201
LOGS: A Language of Group Skills	R. Herman	'85-209
Improving Client-Consultant Relationships: Research-Based Suggestions	D.M. Kellogg	'87-247
Thirty Years of Human Service Education and Training—One Perspective	H.G. Dimock	'87-269
Overview of the SYMLOG System: Measuring Behavior in Groups	R.F. Bales	'88-261

FACILITATION (Continued)

Title	Author(s)	Volume & Page No.
Improving the Use of Behavior Modeling in Communication and Coaching-Skills Training	D.C. Kinlaw	'90-241

RESEARCH

Title	Author(s)	Volume & Page No.
The Message from Research	J.R. Gibb	'74-155
Structured Experiences in Groups: A Theoretical and Research Discussion	R.R. Kurtz	'75-167
Basic Statistics for the HRD Practitioner	J.J. Maiorca	'91-245

INTRODUCTION TO AND CLASSIFICATION
OF RESOURCES

In recent years there has been phenomenal growth in the training and development fields. The availability of materials and services has increased to the point that it is difficult to maintain a current understanding of resources available to the facilitator and consultant.

The classification of the material in the Resources sections of the 1972-1983 *Annuals* and of the resources found in the Professional Development sections of the 1984-1992 *Annuals* is as follows:

Bibliography
Professional Affiliations
International
Personal Growth Approaches
Product Sources

Readers who are familiar with previous editions of the *Reference Guide* will note that the "Book Reviews" classification was eliminated in the 1981 edition. Large-scale, topical book reviews from previous *Annuals* are now listed under the "Bibliography" classification since they are, in effect, annotated bibliographies of books in a particular subject area.

BIBLIOGRAPHY

Title	Author(s)	Volume & Page No.
A Step Toward Definition: *Review of The Addison-Wesley Series on Organization Development*	T. Lyons	'72-266
A Personalized Human Relations Training Bibliography	M. Smith	'73-247
A Bibliography of Small-Group Training, 1973-1974	W.B. Reddy	'75-264
A Reference List for Change Agents	L.E. Pate	'76-241
Humanistic Education: A Review of Books Since 1970	P.A. Schmuck & R.A. Schmuck	'76-265
Values Clarification: A Review of Major Books	J. Goodman	'76-274
Transactional Analysis: A Review of the Literature	H. Capers	'76-280
A Bibliography of Nonverbal Communication	R.W. Rasberry	'77-227
A Bibliography of Small-Group Training, 1974-1976	W.B Reddy and K. Lippert	'77-238
Assertion: The Literature Since 1970	C. Kelley	'77-264
Organization Development: A Review of Recent Books (1973-1976)	M. Sashkin	'77-276
Humanistic and Transpersonal Education: A Guide to Resources	J. Canfield	'78-277
Small-Group Behavior and Development: A Selective Bibliography	G. Hearn	'79-252
A Brief Glossary of Frequently Used Terms in Organization Development and Planned Change	M. Sashkin	'80-249
Career Development: Literature and Resources	H.L. Fromkin & J.D. McDonald	'80-285
Periodicals in Organization Development and Related Fields	S.M. Rosenthal & L.P. Church	'81-259
Annotated Bibliography on Power in Organizations	M. Smith & H.L. Fromkin	'81-269
A Bibliography of Small-Group Training, 1976-1979	W.B. Reddy & K.M. Lippert	'81-284
An Annotated Bibliography and Critique of Reviews of Group Research	R. Stockton	'82-266
Team Building/Team Development: A Reference List	R.C. Diedrich	'83-267

BIBLIOGRAPHY (Continued)

Title	Author(s)	Volume & Page No.
Biofeedback: An Outline of the Literature and Resource Directory (1983 Update)	H. Pikoff	'83-273
A Bibliography of Applications of the Myers-Briggs Type Indicator (MBTI) to Management and Organizational Behavior	J.A. Sample	'84-145
Neurolinguistic Programming: A Resource Guide and Review of the Research	D.W. McCormick	'84-267
Organization Development Resource Guide: A Bibliography	H.H. Johnson	'86-249
An Annotated Bibliography on the Work Force of the Twenty-First Century: Baby Boom and Bust	M.E. Collins	'92-223

PROFESSIONAL AFFILIATIONS

Title	Author(s)	Volume & Page No.
The International Association of Applied Social Scientists	K.D. Benne & S.J. Ruma	'72-141
Alphabet Soup	F. Johnson	'72-231
Growth Centers	W. Swartley	'73-267
AHP Growth Center List	Association for Humanistic Psychology	'74-255
Applied Behavioral Science Consulting Organizations: A Directory		'75-249
AHP Growth Center List, 1976	Association for Humanistic Psychology	'77-252
Graduate Programs in Applied Behavioral Science: A Directory	S. Campbell	'78-229
AHP Growth Center List, 1978		'79-270
Alphabet Soup: 1980	F.P. Johnson	'80-265
Applied Behavioral Science Consulting Organizations: An Updated Directory		'80-271
Growth Center Directory: 1982 Update		'82-217
Graduate Programs in Applied Behavioral Science: An Updated Directory		'82-231

PROFESSIONAL AFFILIATIONS (Continued)

Title	Author(s)	Volume & Page No.
Applied Behavioral Science Consulting Organizations: An Updated Directory		'83-255
Executive Recruiters: A Directory	L. Whitaker	'83-282
Neurolinguistic Programming: A Resource Guide and Review of the Research	D.W. McCormick	'84-272
A Directory of Professional Associations: Human Resource Development and Beyond		'92-175

INTERNATIONAL

Title	Author(s)	Volume & Page No.
Human Relations Training in the UK and Continental Europe	C.L. Cooper	'74-249
Canada's Experience with Human Relations Training	H.G. Dimock	'75-233

PERSONAL GROWTH APPROACHES

Title	Author(s)	Volume & Page No.
Awareness Through Movement	M. Feldenkrais	'75-238
An Introduction to Structural Integration (Rolfing)	R. Pierce	'75-241
What Is Psychosynthesis?		'75-246
Bioenergetic Therapy	P. Katz	'76-235
Hatha Yoga	L.C. Trueblood	'76-238

PRODUCT SOURCES

Title	Author(s)	Volume & Page No.
Games and Simulations: Materials, Sources, and Learning Concepts	B.D. Ruben	'72-235
Media Resources for Human Relations Training	N. Felsenthal	'72-241
Selecting Workshop Sites	T.A. Boone & R.A. Reid	'78-253
Human Relations Films for Group Facilitators	D.L. Smith	'78-260

PRODUCT SOURCES (Continued)

Title	Author(s)	Volume & Page No.
Using a Video System in Human Relations Training		
Video Feedback in Groups and Organizations	D. Francis	'79-239
Selecting an Appropriate Video System	A.R. Davidson	'79-245
Facilitating Simulation Games	M.R. Chartier	'81-247
Training Packages in Stress Management	Human Resource Development Press	'82-259

NAME INDEX

Abraham, E., 175
Ackerman, L.S., 204
Adams, J.D., 50, 186
Adler, N.J., 200
Ahrons, C.R., 87
Akin, G., 45
Albrecht, K.G., 62
Alexander, C.P., 154
Alexander, M., 173, 176, 184
Allen, B.J., Jr., 140
Amesley, C.E., 44
Anderson, D., 70
Anderson, J.P., 204
Anderson, W., 175
Arbes, B.H., 155, 174
Armor, T., 110
Association for Humanistic
    Psychology, 211
Aufrecht, S.E., 127

Bailey, W.J., 37
Baker, H.K., 127
Bales, R.F., 206
Ballard, J., 92, 186
Ballew, A.C., 60, 72, 142
Bancroft, E., 186
Banet, A.G., Jr., 141, 155, 158, 160,
    172, 176, 185, 186, 187, 188, 204,
    206
Barber, W., 152
Barott, J., 31
Bates, R.R., 199, 203
Beamish, G.E.H., 49, 172
Bechtel, D., 136
Beckhard, R., 201
Belforti, R.P., 139
Bell, B., 125
Bellanca, J.A., 148
Bellman, G., 131

Bem, S.L., 177
Benne, K.D., 95, 125, 211
Bennis, W.G., 124, 175, 199
Berger, M.A., 184
Berkowitz, N.H., 107
Berliner, J.P., 87
Berman, L., 32
Bienvenu, M.J., Sr., 172, 176
Blair, D.M., 188
Blake, B., 176
Blanchard, K.H., 174
Blank, W., 175
Blase, J.J., 99, 184
Blau, G., 175
Blizzard, M., 89
Bond, K.M., 105
Boone, T.A., 186, 188, 212
Boshear, W.C., 62, 186
Bova, R.A., 63
Bowdery, K.J., 112
Bowens, H., Jr., 52
Bowers, D.G., 198
Bracey, H., 150
Briner, W., 200
Broskowski, A., 198
Brosseau, M., 125
Brostrom, R., 172
Brown, K.S., 76
Bruce, W.M., 143
Bryant, J.C., 39, 173
Budd, R.W., 88
Buller, P.F., 200
Bunker, B.B., 200
Bunning, R.L., 36, 41, 134, 202
Burchett, T., 103
Burden, 75, 174
Burke, W.W., 124, 172, 200, 205
Burns, F., 173, 175
Burr, A.J., 42

215

TITLE INDEX